How to Declutter Your Mind

Secrets to Stop Overthinking, Relieve Anxiety, and Achieve Calmness and Inner Peace

How to Declutter Your Mind

How to Declutter Your Mind

Table of Contents

Your Free Gifts

As a way of saying thanks for your purchase, I want to offer you a free bonus e-Book called *7 Essential Mindfulness Habits* exclusive to the readers of this book.

To get instant access just go to:

https://theartofmastery.com/mindfulness

Inside the book, you will discover:

- What is mindfulness meditation

- Why mindfulness is so effective in reducing stress and increasing joy, composure, and serenity
- Various mindfulness techniques that you can do anytime, anywhere
- 7 essential mindfulness habits to implement starting today
- Tips and fun activities to teach your kids to be more mindful

Introduction

Our modern lives are as cluttered as they are hectic. There are so many different things demanding our attention at a time. Whether in school or the workforce, there's always someone expecting us to complete an assignment and follow their instructions. We are constantly bombarded with tasks and responsibilities to the point that it can feel like the only rest we get is when we go to sleep at the end of the day. Our personal lives can be just as frantic as our professional ones. Maintaining relationships often cuts into the little free time that we have, and while we may love our friends and family, sometimes keeping up with all of the plans and trying to be available for all of their needs can be as exhausting as work. Our calendars end up packed, and we're often left racing around trying to balance everything on our plates and desperately hoping we don't drop anything.

As a mother of two, I am intimately familiar with just how frantic life can be. I used to feel incredibly overwhelmed at the start of every day just thinking of all I needed to do by the end of it.

I had all of my personal and professional responsibilities, and I also had to worry about my kids. I would race around in the mornings getting them ready and packing their lunches, all while running through a mental list of everything I needed to get done as soon as they were out the door. This left me with next to no time to unwind, which led me to feel anxious a great deal of the time. I was a compulsive overthinker, and my anxieties about my busy, cluttered life would play on repeat behind my eyelids as I tried to get some sleep at night. That doesn't even include how physically cluttered the house was. It wasn't uncommon to walk into a room and trip over some scattered blocks, and both my husband and I had made impulse purchases that ended up sitting on a shelf collecting dust. With so much clutter in my life, I knew I was creating a lot of stress for myself, and I needed to find a way to get things under control.

When our lives and our surroundings are cluttered, our minds are too. Our environment has an impact on our mental state. For example, certain colors can influence us based on their associations. Red is usually associated with passion and movement, so it often makes us feel more active. A small change in the colors of a room or building can affect how we feel at that location.

The same theory is true of the level of clutter in our environments. A neat and tidy room helps us feel more relaxed and allows us to focus on the task at hand because there is nothing to distract ourselves with. On the other hand, a busier environment full of distractions makes it harder for us to focus because it gives us too many different things for our brains to latch onto.

Imagine you're at work, and you have a TV playing in the room. It becomes nearly impossible to concentrate because even if you try to tune it out, the noise and visuals from the TV add to the amount of mental clutter you're experiencing. Even your phone can become a significant distraction due to the high level of clutter in the digital world. A busy schedule and relationships that require a lot of upkeep can impact you in the same way. Too much clutter for too long makes our brains buzz with activity, even when we're trying to focus or rest. If this state persists for too long, we can end up with numerous negative effects such as overthinking, anxiety, tension, and an inability to concentrate.

Knowing all of this, you might be wondering to yourself: What is the solution to reducing overthinking and decreasing anxiety? If environmental and lifestyle clutter create mental clutter, then decluttering our lives will help us declutter our minds.

The idea of reducing clutter takes a page out of the minimalism book. In minimalism, having a cleaner, more organized environment is more than just aesthetically pleasing. It is a more streamlined way to interact with our environment that reduces the number of distractions we encounter in our everyday life. A minimalist environment promotes greater mindfulness by taking the focus away from our surroundings and bringing it back toward ourselves. It becomes easier to navigate our surroundings more purposefully so we can spend less time on distractions and more time on what really matters. Living in a clutter-free household or workspace can help combat procrastination and overthinking as a result.

The concept of minimalism can be extended to the rest of your life. True minimalism means reducing the amount of unnecessary clutter in all aspects of your life, not just in your house. Deal with excessive clutter at work, and reduce the number of unnecessary responsibilities you have so you can focus on the most important ones. Limit the constant influx of non-essential information you receive from social media and other aspects of the digital world. Eliminate toxic relationships that give you anxiety, just like pruning old, misshapen branches from a tree so the tree can continue to grow. You can even start to rewire your brain, improving your mentality and letting go of harmful thoughts that take up space and hold you back. Declutter each area of your life by throwing out the stressful obligations and distractions that are ultimately unnecessary and bring you anxiety. When you live a more minimalist lifestyle and declutter your mind, you can achieve more mental clarity, focus, productivity, and peace.

With *How to Declutter Your Mind*, you will learn the secrets to living a more stress-free and tranquil life even as our modern world becomes busier and busier. You will learn useful strategies for decluttering various aspects of your life, including both your physical surroundings and your lifestyle. Applying these strategies will allow you to make more time for the parts of life that matter most. You will also have more personal time, which will help you relax and reduce any anxiety you might be feeling over deadlines and a crowded schedule.

It is so easy to fall into the trap of going with the flow of the constant hustle and bustle around us. So many people run themselves ragged every day without knowing there's a way out of this exhausting rat race. You can make time for your family and your close friends, all with time left over to pursue a professional life that aligns with your goals and eliminates busywork. Decluttering your life helps you add hours to your day and gives you a healthier, tidier mental state free of intrusive thoughts and worries. Don't waste any more time on pointless tasks and toxic relationships. Start decluttering your mind today so you can have a calmer life and experience true inner peace.

Chapter 1: What Is Mental Clutter?

"Clutter is anything that does not support your better self."—Eleanor Brownn

When a room is cluttered, it's hard to navigate. Things get lost in all of the junk lying around in unorganized piles. There are plenty of items that could be better used somewhere else in the house or thrown away entirely. These items make it difficult to find whatever we're looking for in the room, and they distract us from our intended purpose. Cluttered rooms directly impact our ability to function in the room. We might think about doing some spring cleaning every once in a while, but when we realize just how much work cleaning the room out would be, we tend to shrug and decide it's a task for another day.

A cluttered mind is similar to a cluttered room. Mental clutter is a term used to describe an overabundance of thoughts in our heads that makes it hard to think clearly. These might include thoughts of responsibilities we've given ourselves or taken on for someone else, multiple tasks we try to complete at the same time, feelings we're having trouble working through, trouble with our relationships, too much stimulation from TV or games, or anything else that only serves to distract us from more important thoughts. Like physical clutter, these thoughts pile up and effectively block out more relevant information. We might have trouble remembering important dates or tasks that we were supposed to get done instead of a bunch of small, meaningless tasks that distracted us.

Trying to stay focused on something when our minds are cluttered can feel the same as digging through a huge pile of junk trying to find the one thing we're looking for. It can cause us to feel just as overwhelmed as we would be in a crowded room or while staring at a huge pile of paperwork we have to complete by the end of the day. We have so much to think about that it all becomes too much. This can cause us to feel overworked, stressed, tired, and anxious.

In order to push back against these distracting and destructive feelings, we must target the root of the problem, not its symptoms. A relaxing spa day or a day off from work might relieve some of your stress at the moment, but as soon as you leave the spa or head back to your job the next morning, all of the stress is going to come right back. Instead, we must address the cause of the stress if we want to banish it for good. We need to reduce our mental clutter. To do this, we have to first examine why mental clutter occurs and find the sources of hyperactive thoughts in our lives.

Why Our Brains Become Cluttered

Mental clutter can come from a wide variety of sources. Some people may have a lot of stress from work, but their relationships are fairly relaxing, while others may find that keeping up relationships is more stressful than any job. Most will find at least a small amount of stress from multiple sources. When stress comes at us from many different angles, it is harder for us to deal with it since it feels like everything in our lives is introducing more mental clutter all at once. It's easy to feel overwhelmed, especially if we lack the right coping methods that might otherwise help us sort through and deal with all of the sources of stress.

Mental clutter looks a little different for everyone, but there are a few sources that are frequent offenders for most of us. If it feels like everything is slipping out of our control, we should take a look at these common causes of stress and mental clutter first. Key problems that can lead to mental clutter include a lack of prioritization of tasks, too many insignificant choices, and an equally cluttered environment. We will learn how to manage these problems throughout the book. For now, we will just take a look at how each of them can impact our lives and minds.

An Inability to Prioritize

Imagine that you have a laundry list of tasks to complete by the end of the day. Some have deadlines, and missing those deadlines will have a negative impact on your job performance, relationships with others, or sense of fulfillment. Others have deadlines further into the future, or they have no real consequences for not getting them done, but they are easier tasks. How do you work through your schedule? Do you just start at the top and work your way down? Do you begin with the hardest tasks or those with the nearest deadlines? Or do you pick off the easy tasks first and then find yourself with a mountain of work to rush through at the end of the day?

When there is too much for us to do in one day, we need to learn how to prioritize. Even though every task on our list is there for a reason, not every task has to be finished at the same time, and not every task is as important as the others. If we cannot separate the critical tasks from those that can wait a day or two, or if we choose to do what's easy instead of what's necessary, we will always find ourselves with far too much work and far too little time.

As the world around us places greater demands on our time and attention, mental clutter is becoming more and more common. We are expected to hold a lot of information in our brains at a time, but as we keep piling on responsibilities and distractions, we only increase the chances of sending the whole pile crashing to the ground. Too many responsibilities can cause us to lose sight of those that matter most. If we fail to prioritize the important tasks, we end up performing the easier, less important ones just to relieve mental clutter. This is just a short-term fix, and it only adds to the amount of clutter in the long run as we scramble to finish the tasks we didn't prioritize.

Too Many Decisions

We are inundated with countless decisions every day. These range from meaningless and benign choices to decisions that can change the direction of our lives. Unfortunately, there is little we can do to alleviate the stress of big decisions. Choosing something like your career path or where you want to live takes a lot of thought and care, and while this kind of decision can also be a source of circling thoughts and overthinking, it's not one that can be so easily set aside. However, there are many decisions we make that aren't nearly as important. An overabundance of these smaller, less significant decisions can compound our stress levels and tax our brains.

Think about the small choices you make every day. When you look in your closet in the morning, how long do you spend trying to pick out an outfit? You might try on a few shirts before you find one that looks right, or you might stand in front of your closet like you're waiting for something new to jump out at you. Staring into the fridge when you're looking for a snack is another all-too-common example of indecision. You probably have a few different things you could eat, but you might still feel like none of them really appeal to you. When you're at the grocery store, there are hundreds of products and dozens of brands for each product. Something as simple as choosing a cereal can take you 10 or 15 minutes as you weigh all of the different options, even though you know that if you had any of the boxes at home, you would eat them without complaint. Any decision would be fine, but it becomes all too easy to agonize over choices that ultimately matter little.

Too many choices can even interfere with relaxation time. You might turn on the TV only to flip through channels for half an hour, your eyes glazing over at the sheer number of options available, ensuring that you never settle on something. Rather than feeling relaxed, making a choice can feel less like finally finding something you're excited to watch and more like giving up and settling.

We desire choice, but too many choices can stress us out. We agonize over whether or not we picked the right thing or if there was a better option we passed over. Psychologist Barry Schwartz calls this the "paradox of choice," finding that "increased choice leads to greater anxiety, indecision, paralysis, and dissatisfaction" (Scott & Davenport, 2016, para. 8). More choices should make us happier, but instead, we spend more time worrying, and our thoughts become even more cluttered. We are distracted by thoughts of what could have been if we'd made a different choice, even if little would have changed in the long run. Even worse, too many of these smaller decisions can make it harder to focus on the big ones. The distraction they pose could keep us from taking the time we need to make the right choice when it matters. If we allow ourselves to get too bogged down in the details of less important choices, we will be unable to give the important choices the gravitas they deserve. Instead, they will be shoved to the backs of our minds, buried under mountains of mental clutter.

Cluttered Surroundings

Our environments have a significant impact on our mental states. You can experience the effect for yourself by just imagining yourself in different places. First, picture yourself at work, complete with all of the stresses of your job. Then, picture yourself laying on the beach, the sun beating down on you, and the waves lapping against the shore. Could you feel your shoulders relax a little bit as you went from work to the beach? Did you notice yourself breathing a little easier? If the effect of simply picturing yourself in different locations is this strong, then it is easy to see how being in one location or another can drastically change how tense you are. After all, you probably feel a lot more relaxed at home than you do at work—unless your home environment is just as chaotic and cluttered as your job.

The home should be somewhere safe and relaxing for us. When we allow it to get cluttered, we subconsciously increase our mental clutter as well until we can hardly find peace in our beds. This is true for any overly crowded location we might find ourselves in throughout the day. Clutter affects our brains and bodies, and that's not just because we might stub our toes or trip on a stray object. In fact, "clutter can affect our anxiety levels, sleep, and ability to focus," and it can also "make us less productive, triggering coping and avoidance strategies that make us more likely to snack on junk and watch TV shows" instead of dealing with the actual problem of having too much stuff (Sander, 2019, para. 4-5). When our environments are not conducive to productivity and focus, we have a hard time settling our thoughts long enough to get any work done. We also have trouble feeling fully relaxed when there are so many distractions around us.

Sometimes, it may feel more convenient to have more stuff in our homes, but the comfort that it affords us on the surface is a double-edged sword. Having too many possessions can make us less likely to exert effort. We get comfortable with our lives as they are, and while we may dream of something better, we lack the drive to achieve it because of how convenient our lives already are. We use impulse purchases as sources of temporary happiness instead of working to build a life that is truly fulfilling. This might mean we avoid anything that could jeopardize our comfort, including opportunities to build a better life. Having too much stuff isn't just a financial or physical issue; it is a problem that can completely take over our mindsets and keep us from pursuing what we really care about.

The issue of environmental clutter is something that minimalists have been aware of for a long time. They have frequently preached the benefits of decluttering your environment in order to declutter your thoughts. This same concept can be applied to all of the previous sources of mental clutter. By reducing the amount of time-wasting junk in all areas of our lives, we can slow down our racing thoughts and get rid of mental clutter.

What Does It Mean to Declutter Your Thoughts?

You can declutter your thoughts the same way you might tidy up physically. Think of your mind as a house and each area of your life as a room within that house. If there is too much junk in any one room, that room has to be cleaned up. If all of the rooms have too much clutter, then all of the rooms have to be cleaned, but you can't clean every room at once. Instead, start by examining a single room, or area of your life, and work your way through each area from there.

Sometimes, decluttering means throwing things away. When you're decluttering your thoughts, this might include lowering the number of tasks you burden yourself with each day. "Throw away" any tasks that aren't necessary and don't bring you any sense of enjoyment or fulfillment. You may also need to throw away certain relationships that have grown toxic and harmful to one or both parties. Both of these things are hard, just like throwing out items you've been hoarding, but once you clear your life of unnecessary worries, it will all be worth it.

At other times, decluttering can just mean tidying up and reorganizing. For example, creating a schedule for yourself can help you complete activities on time and stick to priority tasks above all else. Adjusting your schedule can also help you free up more time for family and friends. Reorganizing physically can help too, whether you're rearranging your closet or completely revamping the furniture arrangement in your living room. You aren't throwing anything away, but by packing things into organized boxes and lists, you're still opening up your schedule and living a more relaxed lifestyle.

As we continue through the book, you will learn how to systematically clean out each room of your mental house. As you do, you will learn what really matters and what you can live without. You will start to prioritize your responsibilities, cut back on unnecessary decision-making, and declutter your physical environment alongside your thoughts. This process will allow you to avoid the detrimental effects of too much mental clutter, helping you lead a focused, committed life full of only the things that matter most to you.

Chapter Takeaways

This chapter dealt with basic information about the idea of mental clutter. In this chapter, you learned:

- The term "mental clutter" refers to the idea of cleaning out unnecessary sources of strife and stress from your life.

- There are several common causes of mental clutter, including trouble prioritizing responsibilities, stressing over small decisions, and crowded surroundings.

- To declutter your thoughts is to remove or lessen the sources of mental clutter you encounter every day.

In the next chapter, we'll take a look at all of the ways mental clutter holds you back.

Chapter 2: How Mental Clutter Works Against You

"You can't reach for anything new if your hands are full of yesterday's junk."—Louise Smith

You now understand what mental clutter is, but you might not yet be sold on the idea of reducing it. After all, it involves rehauling a great deal of your life, and this can take a lot of effort. You might be asking yourself: Is all of this really necessary? How bad can mental clutter really be?

Though it may seem harmless in small amounts, mental clutter is surprisingly counterproductive to living a fulfilling life. If you allow clutter to persist, you invite a whole host of physical and mental effects that could otherwise be avoided.

It's no secret that clutter is troublesome, but is it really dangerous? When it comes to mental clutter, the effects can be more worrying than you would first think. Clutter works against us because it changes the way our brains process the world around us. We tend to gravitate toward organization. We function best when our environments are suited for our goals. When we work, we want a clean environment free of anything that would pull our attention away from our task. It's much easier to get some work done if we're at a desk that is free of clutter than it is if the TV remote is within our reach and there are scattered stacks of papers everywhere. The same is also true of mental clutter. If we're thinking about a conversation that we had yesterday that didn't go as planned or we're worried about completing all of the tasks on our mental list for the day, our thoughts may drift from our work more often than they should.

An inability to focus on anything for long ensures that we can't reach our full potential. It takes patience and care to work toward our long-term goals, neither of which we can achieve if we can't concentrate. When we allow clutter to distract us, we effectively sabotage ourselves. Of course, a lack of focus is a more obvious symptom of the mental clutter issue, but it's not the only one. There are many other effects of living a cluttered life that can be just as if not more damaging.

Effects of a Cluttered Life

Distraction is just one part of the burden of clutter. Living and working in cluttered environments, either physically or in terms of our lifestyle, is more likely to make us stressed and anxious. We feel trapped and restless, which can trick us into believing that we're in danger. This kind of prolonged stress can have serious results.

Another issue comes from the tension between instant gratification and delayed gratification. If we fill our lives with clutter in the form of impulse purchases or endlessly scrolling through social media instead of putting our phones down and doing something more constructive with our time, we give in to the pull of instant gratification. We choose an easy, simple task over a more complex one. This subconsciously trains us to repeat the same behavior, which can seriously get in the way of our ability to achieve long-term success.

These two impacts, stress and instant gratification, show us just how detrimental mental clutter can be to our mental and physical health. By understanding how each of these impacts works against us, we can start to understand the value of decluttering our lives.

Clutter and Stress

Stress has often been referred to as "the silent killer." Some people only experience stress briefly and periodically. This is not so bad. Our bodies are designed to manage brief bursts of stress by entering into what is commonly known as fight-or-flight mode. In this mode, our reflexes are heightened, our blood pressure and heart rate increase, and we're ready to act. In small doses, like when we're staying up late to work on a big project or if we have to run from a dangerous animal, we can process this stress without a problem. The danger eventually goes away, and our fight-or-flight response goes away with it.

Chronic stress is a much greater problem. We get stuck in the mentality that we should be running or hiding from something, even if we're not facing life-threatening circumstances. If our lives are hectic and we're always on edge, the 'threat' our minds are perceiving doesn't go away. It sticks around, leaving us saddled with high stress. Without good coping strategies or any way to decrease the amount of stress in our life, we constantly feel a low-level threat that we can't do anything about. This chronic stress can lead to serious health issues.

Stress leaves you feeling on edge and tense. Excessive tension for a long time can leave you with persistent soreness. Try flexing the muscles in your arm, then hold them that way for a few seconds. When you relax, you'll feel a minor ache that should go away quickly. Now, imagine you carry low-level tension around with you all of the time. That minor ache becomes a major one, and it doesn't go away nearly as quickly because you are never able to fully relax.

Long-term stress can also lead to high blood pressure, which increases your risk of a heart attack, stroke, or heart disease. Your heart works double or triple as hard as it usually does, which puts a lot of strain on your body. Stress can also interfere with your digestive system. It has been linked to higher rates of diabetes, eating disorders, and obesity, as well as conditions such as Crohn's disease, ulcerative colitis, and irritable bowel syndrome (American Brain Society, 2019, para. 10). These conditions range from uncomfortable to quite dangerous to your health.

But what does all of this have to do with clutter? Surely a busy schedule and a messy room can't be connected to these serious consequences, can they? Unfortunately, many studies have found that clutter can indeed act as a stressor that creates chronic, persistent stress in our lives. A research study on mothers found "the levels of the stress hormone cortisol were higher in mothers whose home environment was cluttered" (Sander, 2019, para. 11). The more clutter that surrounds us, the higher our cortisol levels, and the more likely we are to experience the damaging effects of chronic stress. To fix this problem, we must go further than temporary solutions like taking a day off. We must deal with the issue at its roots, meaning we have to reduce the number of sources of stress we are exposed to every day. If we don't, we could be facing serious health issues.

How Clutter Holds You Back

Think about the most cluttered room in your house. What kind of objects are in it? When you bought these objects, were you thinking about how they would help you in the long term, or were you just trying to fulfill a short-term need? Were they carefully thought-out purchases, or were they impulse buys? Chances are that if you had taken the time to really consider if you needed each item or not, you wouldn't have ended up with such a cluttered room in the first place. Clutter comes from the accumulation of things we don't need, which are often things we only bought to solve a short-term problem and haven't gotten around to throwing away yet.

Now think about a cluttered aspect of your life, whether it's part of your professional or personal life. Did you really think through all of the decisions you made that brought you to this point? When you chose your job, were you thinking about how it would help you achieve your future career goals, or did you just need something to pay the bills, even if the job wasn't particularly fulfilling? When you decided not to talk about the elephant in the room with someone you're close to, did you consider the future ramifications, or were you only trying to avoid the temporary discomfort?

Many of the greatest mistakes we make in life come from a place of trying to avoid pain and only looking for what is the most enjoyable. We may think that this causes the least amount of harm in the short term, but when you look at the long-term effects, these kinds of choices often end up doing more harm than good. For example, when you chose not to talk about that difficult subject with a friend, family member, or partner, you probably did it to spare their feelings. However, if the situation persists, the relationship might grow stilted and distant as the two of you dance around the topic, or you might become more frustrated because of something they don't even know is bothering you. Maybe you chose your current job for no other reason than the payment, not thinking about how it would fit into your plans for the future. If your job is draining and isn't in the field you want to pursue, it could be contributing to your mental clutter and exhaustion. As the clutter builds up from short-sighted decisions, it could become harder to recognize that there's another way.

Pursuing instant gratification and making impulsive decisions interfere with your ability to think critically about your choices. Skipping a healthy lunch and grabbing fast food might taste good at the moment, but it does no favors for your health. The longer you repeat the behavior, the harder it becomes to change your ways. This is true for all habits that work against you instead of helping you pursue your goals. Building up clutter from poor decision-making just reinforces the bad decisions. It's harder to make your lunch if you're used to getting fast food and haven't cooked in a while. It's harder to find a job that's personally fulfilling if you've convinced yourself your current one is safer, and it's harder to finally broach that uncomfortable topic with a friend if it's been tainting the relationship for months.

When you start shifting your focus toward your future rather than settling for whatever causes the least amount of discomfort at the moment, your fear of discomfort starts to fade. Cluttered surroundings and a cluttered life might keep you comfortable on the surface, but stress and anxiety sit just underneath the surface level of comfort. Additionally, this sense of paper-thin comfort keeps you just complacent enough that you don't really feel motivated enough to make the necessary changes in your life. If you can learn to let go of the things that make your life so cluttered, even when it's hard or the results are uncertain, you will live a more fulfilling life overall. Reducing the clutter lets you start seeing the forest for the trees. It becomes easier to let go of the things you're keeping around that serve no purpose, giving you greater peace of mind.

Chapter Takeaways

In this chapter, you learned about the damaging effects that too much clutter can have on your mind and your life. The lessons you learned in this chapter include:

- A life full of clutter can distract you from what's important.

- Being in cluttered environments can create higher levels of cortisol, a stress hormone, in your body.

- Stress can lead to significant health problems like gastrointestinal issues, aches and pains, and heart disease.

- Continued clutter makes it harder to focus on achieving your goals and gets you into the habit of thinking short-term instead of long-term.

Next, we'll compare these negative effects to all of the positive effects that you can enjoy if you rid your life of clutter.

Chapter 3: The Benefits of Decluttering Your Mind

"When we throw out the physical clutter, we clear our minds. When we throw out the mental clutter, we clear our souls."—Gail Blanke

As we learned in the previous chapter, distraction, stress, and caving to instant gratification are some of the negative impacts of clutter. The more stressed we are, the more likely we are to experience anxiety and overthinking. If we want to eliminate these troublesome and sometimes dangerous side effects, we need to declutter our minds.

Decluttering your mind isn't easy. It can take a lot of work, and it may require you to make some difficult choices. You are going to have to choose the hard road over the easy road sometimes. But when you know the benefits that await you when you rid your life of clutter, it becomes so much easier to make the right choice.

Mental clutter undermines you at every turn. As long as your lifestyle is cluttered, filling your daily schedule with busywork and tasks that don't align with your goals, you will experience the negative effects. Trying to achieve success, whatever success means to you, is difficult when you spend your time in a cluttered house or cluttered workspace dealing with a cluttered mind. To declutter your mind is to lessen the impact of these negative effects and, ultimately, to remove their power over you altogether. Decluttering helps you deal with the problem at its source. You reduce the number of things in your life that contribute to stress and stop using impulse purchases to manage your moods. Through this, you are able to free up time that you would have otherwise spent either completing meaningless tasks or worrying about these sources of stress. Decluttering your mind gives you more time for rest, and it can significantly improve your mentality. These are positive effects that are well worth any amount of effort required to achieve them.

How Decluttering Your Mind Supports Your Continued Growth

If you've ever done spring cleaning, you know what it feels like to transform a mess of old junk, piles of clothes, and other clutter into a neat and tidy room. The work is a little tiring, and you're sure to get a good workout from it. You might spend an entire day throwing things out and rearranging what's left, or you might break it up and tackle the work over multiple days or weeks. No matter how you tackle it, there's a sense of satisfaction that comes from a job well done. When you look around you and see everything in its place, free of anything that had only been gathering dust while it went unused, you feel good about what you've accomplished. It's like you're giving yourself an opportunity to start over, and as long as you keep things clean and avoid buying things you don't need again, you won't have to repeat the process next spring.

Since mental decluttering follows the same principles as minimalistic interior design, it can bring us similar results. When we declutter our minds, we give ourselves a greater sense of freedom. Our schedules open up, our thoughts are free of distractions, and the restless buzzing of our thoughts at the back of our head is quieted. Without mental clutter, we can feel more at peace than we have for years. Alongside all of these benefits, we also make it easier for ourselves to focus on the future rather than lingering in the past. As we begin thinking about what's next for us, we can start to clear out any responsibilities that don't help us achieve our goals, making us more efficient and more relaxed at the same time.

Free Up Your Schedule

A cluttered schedule full of assignments and deadlines isn't conducive to a good work-life balance or good mental health. We can only deal with so many tasks at a time. If we are constantly running around without any downtime, we're only going to grow more exhausted each day. Eventually, we start to feel burned out. Even doing small tasks becomes almost impossible, and everything takes much more effort than it ever did before. Burnout can decimate our ability to be productive and lead us into the trap of procrastination. When we already have a busy schedule, procrastinating makes things even worse. Mental clutter mounts as we think of all of the things we need to do, but we lack the motivation necessary to get any of them done.

When we begin decluttering our schedules, the wave of work that threatens to overwhelm us grows smaller by the day. Instead of a mountain of tasks waiting for us each day, we start doing only those that really need to get done. This allows us to manage our time better and gives us more free time. Decompression is just as important as getting work done. If we are constantly stressed, the quality of our work will suffer. Freeing up our schedules and giving ourselves breaks lets us feel relaxed and rejuvenated. Rather than making us 'lazy,' this encourages us to get more work done. We are no longer distracted by small tasks, nor do we constantly feel burned out. Because of this, we have the energy and motivation we need to tackle the important things we've been putting off. The quality of our work improves, and we have more time available to share with family and friends.

Decluttering can help us improve our mentalities about work too. When you're constantly busy, every bit of new work feels like a chore. You dread getting new assignments and responsibilities because you have to find a way to fit them in with everything that's already on your to-do list. When you drop some of the unimportant tasks and give yourself less to do each day, any new task feels less like a burden and more like an opportunity. We start feeling excited by work and other activities again because we feel like we're making a choice of whether or not to take them on, rather than having them forced upon us. When we are in greater control of our lives and our daily schedules, even the hard tasks become something we're doing because we're passionate about the outcome. We have made the deliberate choice to commit to the task knowing that it really matters to us whether or not it gets done. This feeling of self-empowerment makes difficult activities a lot more bearable.

Eliminate Circling Thoughts

When our minds are cluttered, we give ourselves a lot to think about. Whether we ruminate on the busy day we just had, think about what awaits us tomorrow, or simply get distracted by our environment, our thoughts may grow to be loud and disruptive. It's hard to focus on anything when these thoughts clutter our minds. We might find ourselves drifting and hardly paying attention to what's in front of us. This ensures we can't focus our full concentration on anything, whether we're trying to work on something or relax. We end up doing everything by half measures, sabotaging ourselves with the thoughts that won't stop circling in our heads. If we're working, our train of thought falters periodically, and the quality of our work may suffer. If we're trying to relax, reminders of the responsibilities we're avoiding keep intruding upon what should be a leisurely activity, causing stress to return full-force.

Circling thoughts are especially troublesome when they follow you to bed. If you're someone who frequently finds yourself overthinking, you've probably kept yourself up with your worries before. Every time you try to close your eyes and clear your mind, another source of anxiety intrudes upon your thoughts. You think about something that happened earlier in the day that didn't go as planned or something you need to do tomorrow that's giving you stress already. Thoughts bounce around in your skull, ensuring that every time you nearly fall asleep, you are jolted awake again. This may even become a nightly occurrence if things in your life don't slow down. Overthinking can lead to chronic insomnia, which limits the amount of sleep you get each night and leaves you feeling almost perpetually tired. You don't want to float through the next day in a barely-there haze, especially if you've got a schedule that's as cluttered as your thoughts.

Decluttering your mind helps you calm these circling thoughts so you can focus during the day and get better rest at night. When your mind isn't constantly jumping from one thing to another, always reminding you of all your sources of worry, it is much easier to settle your thoughts. Instead of lying in bed all night staring up at your ceiling, you will be able to relax and fall asleep more readily. This will leave you feeling refreshed and ready to go the next day, more than capable of handling whatever life throws at you without slipping back into mental clutter.

Trade Anxiety for Peace and Calmness

Too much clutter makes us anxious. If this clutter is physical, we can feel like we're trapped, forcing our way through our homes rather than following the natural flow of each room. It's uncomfortable to pick our way around a cluttered room, and it requires us to think about where we're going more than a clean room would. On top of this, if we keep items around because we believe we will need them again at some unknown future point, we likely do so out of a form of anxiety. We worry that we will be unprepared for the future if we don't have 20 different charging cables in our desk or if we don't keep the clothes that we haven't worn in years but "might wear again someday." Maybe we feel anxious about the money we spent on items that ultimately turned out to be less useful than we thought, and we're only keeping them around out of this same sense of anxiety. Rather than keeping our minds at peace, however, living in a cluttered environment leaves us with mounting worries and fears that are often unrealistic or unnecessary.

A cluttered schedule and mind give us this same form of clutter anxiety. If we're always racing to keep up with everything we need to do today, we never give ourselves a chance to relax and unwind. If we allow our thoughts to circle and spiral into negativity at every turn, we start looking at everything through a negative lens, which only makes our anxiety worse.

Decluttering is the solution to these problems. With a cleaner living space, a less demanding schedule, and no more circling thoughts, many of the everyday sources of anxiety we encounter will vanish too. Without them, we will feel more comfortable and peaceful. Rather than bustling around, we can take our time with tasks and give them the attention they deserve. This eliminates any worries about a poorly done job. It also takes a load off our shoulders and encourages us to slow down and breathe. Less mental clutter helps us feel peaceful and dispels many different sources of worry that would otherwise hold us back.

Focus on Your Future

Many of the things that clutter our minds are relics of the past. They sit on shelves in our mind collecting dust, even as they continue to give us anxiety and stress. Think about how many items you have in your home that you just haven't used in years. Unless you've made a dedicated effort to go minimalist, you probably have plenty of things you bought with the best of intentions but never ended up using. Now, you might only keep them around out of a sense of obligation. You made an unnecessary purchase in the past, you reason, so the least you can do is keep it until it becomes useful again. However, the item in question typically never ends up becoming useful again. It only takes up space.

Past decisions in many different forms can continue to haunt us long after we make them. If we're unhappy with our job but we've had it for many years, we might rationalize it by pointing out that we've had it forever and it would be tough to get a new one. Because we have convinced ourselves we are comfortable as we are, we cling to the past, unwilling to hunt for a job that would make us happier. Old relationships can be negative forces in our lives too. Not all old friendships are bad, of course— we might have some friends we made in childhood whose company we still enjoy, and that's fine—but sometimes, we continue a friendship only because we've had it for a long time. If the relationship is draining rather than fulfilling, we should ask ourselves why we insist on maintaining it. Learning to let go of toxic relationships is a huge step toward decluttering our minds. It isn't always easy, but if we remain stuck in these harmful relationships, we will never be able to move forward with our lives.

Impulse purchases kept around for years, dead-end jobs, toxic relationships, and other sources of clutter are all things of the past. They keep us trapped in place, connecting us to our old lives and preventing us from escaping to a cleaner, less cluttered life. We have to learn to let go of these things before we can move forward. We must keep with us only those things that are positive, healthy forces in our lives and throw out everything else. Otherwise, we will always be looking backward instead of forward. By ridding our lives of clutter, we can start focusing on our future, not our past.

Is Decluttering Really Effective?

The amazing effects of decluttering might sound too good to be true. You may also be wondering to yourself: Is clutter really this powerful? Can decluttering actually help me make these changes?

It may be hard to see just how effective decluttering can be in your life if you picture it only as throwing away some old junk or if you think decluttering only happens on a mental level. You might picture decluttering as something as simple as a meditation exercise; perhaps you will clear your mind, but all of the clutter will still be there when the meditation ends. However, while meditation might be one part of your decluttering strategy, it shouldn't be the only one. Decluttering doesn't just occur in your mind. It occurs in all aspects of your life.

Clutter is present in many different areas of our lives, so we must declutter each of these areas. Decluttering is a promise you make to yourself to rid your life of everything holding you back. It doesn't stop at just donating a few piles of unworn clothes, and it's not as temporary as a vacation away from your busy life. If you declutter your life, the effects are permanent. When you experience these effects for yourself, you will have no desire to clutter your life all over again and go back to the way things were before. You will start making decisions with more forethought, and you will subconsciously make choices that keep your life free of unnecessary clutter. This will help you feel freer as well.

Decluttering is most effective because it helps you focus on the most important parts of your life. If you find yourself caught up in activities that don't benefit you, decluttering helps you let these activities go. You throw out everything that doesn't align with your desires and goals, whether this is as small of a change as finally getting rid of old clothes that no longer fit or as big of a change as pursuing a new career path. Through this process, you find out what matters to you and what you want to achieve with your life. You also have the time and desire to work toward these goals. Decluttering is so powerful because it allows you to become more in control of your life and gives you all of the tools you need to turn your life around for the better.

Chapter Takeaways

This chapter explained how decluttering your mind can help you. In this chapter, you learned:

- Too much clutter keeps you from becoming the best person you can be.

- Decluttering will help you reduce the amount of work you are expected to do each day and cut your to-do list down to only the necessary tasks.

- With less clutter, racing thoughts will slow down, and you will experience more peace and calmness.

- From this new perspective, you can start working toward goals that are truly important to you.

In the following chapter, we'll examine how our brains function and why we're seemingly predisposed to mental clutter.

Chapter 4: Decluttering Your Brain

"Keeping baggage from the past will leave no room for happiness in the future."—Wayne L. Misner

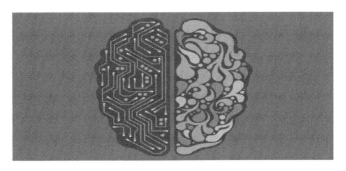

We've spent the last two chapters exploring the idea of mental decluttering and examining why it's a worthwhile endeavor. Now, we're going to start taking the necessary steps to declutter our lives, and through this process, we'll also declutter our minds. From this point on, we will focus on specific areas of our lives and take a look at some actionable advice that we can use to significantly reduce mental clutter. Since clutter affects our thoughts so severely, it only makes sense to start by decluttering our brains.

Our brains are complicated, and even scientists don't know everything about exactly how they function. Chances are you know little about the intricate processes that take place in your head every day. While it can be an intimidating topic, getting a better understanding of our brains can help us see how mental clutter becomes a problem and what we can do to stop it.

First, we'll start with a bit of background knowledge on how our brains work. Our brains control many different functions, and most of them happen without our conscious knowledge. Our brains are connected to our entire bodies. They are responsible for controlling our bodies' automatic processes, like breathing, even though we don't have to think about breathing in order to do it. Our brains are also primarily responsible for responding to stimuli that we encounter in our environments or in our bodies. What affects the mind affects the body, and vice versa; this is because the brain is so thoroughly connected to the rest of our body.

Our minds are hardwired to pick up on all stimuli in our environments. We notice and react to all kinds of things without realizing it. Thousands of years ago, we needed to have such a responsive brain to survive in our environments. Picking up on small details was a matter of life or death. Even today, we still respond somewhat similarly. We might hear a dog angrily barking in the distance and think nothing of it, but our brains pick up on the sound and label it as a potential danger. In response to the stressor, our muscles might tense a bit, and our blood pressure might increase, even though we're not in any immediate danger. These responses occur on such a minute level that you probably won't notice them unless you have a phobia of dogs, but they occur all the same. Still, this is just a minor, acute stressor, so it has little impact on our long-term behavior. The real issues appear when we experience chronic stress.

How Our Brains Process Chronic Stress

Chronic stress is different from acute stress. Our brains have much more trouble managing stress the longer it occurs. This is because our brains become almost overactive, and we have trouble "turning them off" and tuning out our automatic responses. We continue to react to stresses like clutter even if they pose little to no danger simply because that is how we are wired. A cluttered environment and lifestyle make it harder for us to focus and provide many different distractions for our brains to react to, which can overload us. If we are always moving and never get the rest we so desperately need, we can overtax our brains, causing us to experience stress and anxiety more frequently.

Think of the kind of bad mood you experience when you don't get enough sleep. This is because your brain didn't get the rest it needed to function optimally the next day. We are incredibly adaptive and reactive; filling our lives with clutter or overexerting our brains only leads to chronic stress. Over time, the effects of this stress build up and make it harder for us to react to our environments with anything other than stress.

Adaptive Thinking

The incredible adaptability of our brains allows us to react to nearly any situation with only minor hesitation. Typically, adaptability is great. It helps us survive in environments that would otherwise be inhospitable for us, whether this is because we live somewhere extremely hot or cold or because we've entered a new cultural or social environment. Our brains pick up on cues from these environments, and we learn how to react differently than we would under other circumstances. Our ancestors adapted to colder temperatures by creating and wearing clothing to insulate themselves from the cold. Now, we have socialized ourselves to almost always wear clothing in public. This, too, is an adaptation that has been passed down through the generations. A similar type of adaptation occurs if we travel to a different country and try to integrate ourselves into the culture. It takes us some time to catch on to what others are doing, but before we know it, we're acting as if we have lived there our whole lives.

It's important to note that adapting to our environments often has lifelong effects on our behaviors. For example, someone might maintain an accent from the country they grew up in for the rest of their life just because it was how everyone around them sounded when they were learning to talk. If you take a vacation to another country and don't spend long there, you will probably default to the customs of your home country in most situations unless you have been taught to act differently, and even then, it will be a conscious choice to practice the new behavior rather than an automatic response. We can learn and change our behaviors over time if we so choose, but once we have taught ourselves to think one way, it's not so easy to shake the habit.

At this point, you might be asking yourself: What exactly does all of this have to do with clutter again? Clutter is just another type of environment, which means our brains can adapt to it the same way they adapt to everything else. The circuits in our brain are 'plastic,' which means that if we experience the same situation for a while, our thought patterns will shift to accommodate it. These circuits can be "remodeled by stress to change the balance between anxiety, mood control, memory, and decision-making" (McEwen, 2012, para. 1). Changes in our thought patterns caused by clutter and stress are difficult to reverse. These changes are often maladaptive, frequently rewiring us to poorly tolerate extensive stress without developing any meaningful coping mechanisms. The longer we spend in stressful environments, the more our brains become used to this kind of pressure and the more trouble we have effectively resetting our brains.

The plasticity of our brains means that we might completely change the way we think without noticing the shift in our thoughts. When this happens, it's even harder to undo the change since we have become so swept up in our new mindsets that we forget that we have changed at all. This is most dangerous when we start developing a bias toward negative thinking.

Why We're Wired to Think Negatively

Have you ever experienced that one thing that turns a great day into an awful one? You might have had a perfectly fine morning and afternoon, but one bad experience at work or one argument with a family member could turn the whole day on its head. Rather than thinking you had an average day, you might start to believe that you had a terrible day, even though only one or two things went wrong.

This line of thinking can be expanded to your life as a whole. You've likely had both good and bad experiences, but sometimes, it's hard to see the good ones behind the bad ones. You might look back on the last year of your life and think, "That was a bad year," forgetting all of the good times you shared with friends and family along the way. There are certainly some years that are better than others, but there are always some positives to balance out the negatives. However, you have probably noticed that the bad things stand out in your mind much more than the good ones. Why is it that all of the good things that happen become discounted when we encounter minor bad things?

This phenomenon is known as negativity bias. Just like our ability to pick up on small cues in our environments that drastically affect how we interact with them, negativity bias may have developed back when our ancestors needed to avoid threats in their environments. It was more beneficial for us to always be on the lookout for the next bad thing. As psychology and neuroscience professor Barbara Fredrickson explains, "Negativity bias is nature's way of assuring that we don't get lulled into complacency and succumb to avoidable dangers" (Gould, 2019, para. 5). We might not live in environments with the same level of physical danger anymore, but our brains are still wired to fixate on sources of negativity. Everyday sources of stress can make our attitudes much worse and increase the otherwise minor effects of stressful experiences. We elevate them above the everyday positive events until all we can see is negativity.

As you might imagine, this does no favors for our mentalities. If we're always looking for the next thing to aggravate us or always thinking about the last frustrating encounter we had, our mindsets will suffer. Over time, we start to convince ourselves that this persistent negativity is normal and even beneficial. We become increasingly pessimistic, ready to rule everything as a potentially bad experience before we've even tried it. This makes us more set in our ways and can interfere with trying to make a positive change in our lives because we're not willing to take a risk, having already decided it will end badly for us. There are ways to push back against this negativity bias, like mentally reframing a negative event and recognizing that it is only a small part of an otherwise good day, but it takes some time to train our brains away from this thought pattern.

Thanks to negativity bias, our brains multiply the stressful effects of clutter far past what they would otherwise be. A busy schedule or an argument with a friend takes up space in our minds. Even if we try to distract ourselves and forget our worries, the ever-present clutter finds its way into our thoughts. With every new, unfortunate event, the clutter in our minds grows. Eventually, mental clutter itself becomes a source of negativity that interferes with our ability to destress and calm our minds. Negativity from mental clutter overwhelms any positive experiences we might have that day, and we start thinking of every day as a bad day, even if nothing particularly upsetting happened. Our minds are full of negative thoughts, and we start to lose sight of the sources of positivity and optimism in our lives.

In order to reverse the effects of negativity bias, we must work to undermine the clutter that causes our brains to overreact. By doing so, we give our brains fewer sources of negativity to latch onto, which means our thoughts become less cluttered. We must also look at other aspects of our lives that might be affecting our psyche and cluttering our brains and take proactive steps to address these issues.

Other Factors That Affect Our Psyches

Negativity bias is just one of the many factors that can have a detrimental impact on our psyches and increase clutter in our brains. If we want to effectively reduce clutter, we need to address all possible sources. These include things you may have experienced in the past, your current living situation, and events in your life that may cause stress levels that are higher than usual. By considering and addressing each of these factors, you can start to declutter your brain in a comprehensive, full-body way.

Low Self-Esteem

Many self-help books are full of advice about loving yourself. This is for a good reason; having high self-esteem makes it a lot easier to make sweeping changes to your life. Believing that you can do something is the first step to getting it done. If you look at all of the amazing things others are doing and decide you'll never be as successful as they are, you aren't going to be nearly as committed to making and sticking with a positive change. On the other hand, if you wholeheartedly believe that you are a confident and capable person who can and will succeed, you will keep looking for different solutions to every problem that you come across until you find one that works.

People with high self-esteem tend to take failure and misfortune better than those who lack self-confidence. Rather than feeling completely defeated, their confidence in themselves and their abilities allows them to bounce back and start looking for a solution to their problems rather than wallowing in their regrets. If you lack self-esteem, you are more likely to spend time blaming yourself for the unfortunate situation instead of spending that time trying to rebound from it. The more negative thoughts you direct toward yourself, the more your mental clutter grows. You may also find it hard to make significant changes in your life because you don't believe in your own ability to improve your current situation. Without self-esteem, you can easily trap yourself in a lifestyle that breeds mental clutter simply because you are too afraid to take the steps necessary to reduce the clutter.

Improving your self-esteem is tricky, and not every method will work for everyone. Some general guidelines include making an effort to try new things and spending time with people who care about you. Both of these can help you internalize the belief that you are capable and loved. Trying new things shows you that you can grow and that even if you aren't great at something at first, you can improve your skills, which pushes back against the self-defeating attitude. Spending time with loved ones reminds you that others care about you and that you are worthy of their friendship. If you catch yourself thinking negatively about yourself, adding to your mental clutter, reframe these thoughts and counter them with things you like about yourself. Improving your self-esteem gradually removes negative thoughts that are only taking up space in your mind. As your self-esteem grows, your anxiety and erratic thoughts will often calm down as well, letting you live a more peaceful and positive life.

Past Traumas

Traumatic events can follow us long after the cause of our trauma is gone from our lives. Even though we are no longer in the dangerous or stressful situation, we still feel its lasting impression on our psyches from time to time. We might be reminded of the event while doing something completely benign, or we might find ourselves unable to do certain things that remind us of our trauma. This is nothing to be ashamed of, but it can still be a source of frustration and mental clutter if we don't have sufficient coping mechanisms in place.

If left unresolved, past traumatic experiences can continue to interfere with our lives in unexpected ways. Trauma can affect our mental health, making low self-esteem and self-critical thoughts more common. These thoughts may circle and multiply in our heads, especially if we fall prey to our negativity bias. The more our traumas interfere with our lives, the more mental clutter we experience.

Trauma can also affect your behavior patterns. If you are used to people in your life criticizing you, you may put up with a toxic relationship for longer than you should. You might always be willing to give the other person the benefit of the doubt, even if you know deep down that they don't deserve it. Alternatively, if you experienced poverty, you might become more likely to hoard because you are reluctant to throw anything away. It can feel like you are wasting things, even when keeping them around and letting them clutter your house is doing you more harm than good. Financial troubles can also keep you stuck in a job you don't enjoy, even if you now have enough money to live comfortably, just because you remember what it was like to have little to your name. There are many other kinds of traumas that might contribute to clutter in their own way. If you feel like your traumatic experience is creating clutter and standing in the way of a better life for yourself and your family, you may need to seriously consider addressing and working through the trauma before proceeding with the decluttering process.

Managing trauma is not a one-size-fits-all process. Sometimes, you may need to seek professional help from a licensed therapist or psychiatrist. Other times, you may only need the support and reassurance of your friends and family. Choose the method that best helps you develop coping strategies for your trauma. Keep in mind that trauma may reappear over time, and you may not ever completely stop thinking about past events. But if you can find ways to calm your thoughts and reduce the mental clutter that you would otherwise experience, you will be able to avoid a great deal of overthinking and stress.

Current Life Events

Big life events can be incredibly disruptive. We are often completely unprepared for these unusual situations, and they tend to take up a lot of space in our minds. This is especially true if we experience a hardship or misfortune that causes our thoughts to spiral and creates clutter in our brains. Events like the passing of a loved one, the end of a relationship, a health scare, or the unexpected loss of a job or other source of financial security can leave you mentally reeling. It's hard to focus on much of anything when you are in the middle of a crisis. The grieving period that follows these events can be incredibly difficult. You may have difficulty processing your emotional reaction to these events. Your thoughts may constantly circle back to the event, distracting you from whatever you were trying to focus on and forcing your brain to work overtime. This creates a significant amount of mental clutter.

Even positive events can be the source of a lot of clutter. For example, if you're getting married, you're going to have a lot to think about all of the time. You'll need to choose a date, create the guest list, pick out a dress or suit, decide on the venue, arrange for catering, and complete a hundred other tasks before the big day. Anxieties about each of these tasks getting done can create a ton of mental clutter, and if you don't know how to clear your mind and get some rest, the clutter can distract you day and night. Other events like getting a new job, moving, and welcoming a new member into the family can also be sources of clutter, even though they are also happy events.

Dealing with these kinds of stressful events is largely dependent on finding ways to cope with the fallout. Make sure you have an opportunity to breathe and adjust and allow yourself to feel whatever emotions you are feeling because suppressing them only leads to more mental clutter. Sometimes, it's necessary to give yourself time to either heal from an especially unexpected loss or readjust to a new situation. Keep trying to ground yourself whenever you feel your thoughts spiraling, and seek out professional help when necessary.

A Chaotic Lifestyle

Our daily habits and lifestyles can influence our mindsets. If we are used to leading busy lives with no downtime, we start to develop a mindset that prioritizes constant work and doesn't leave any time for proper relaxation. As a result, we only end up running around more, convinced that staying busy is better than getting meaningful work done. We end up leading cluttered lives that create clutter in our brains.

Throughout the rest of the book, we will discuss methods for removing clutter in our lives. These methods include managing our responsibilities, eliminating unnecessary tasks from our daily schedules, reducing sources of distraction in the home and workplace, ridding our lives of detrimental relationships, and changing the way we approach the digital world. Making alterations in each of these areas will help us transform the chaos in our lives into something more orderly, which will allow us to live a life free from mental clutter.

How to Rewire Your Brain, Declutter, and Be Happier

Making changes to our lifestyles and avoiding unnecessary stressful events is only one part of the puzzle that is decluttering our minds. Sometimes, we are able to change the situation we are in. Other times, we are unable to leave a job we hate, cannot let go of a stressful responsibility, or have no way to avoid an event that brings us a lot of stress. In these situations, if we cannot control the source of our stress, then we must focus on the only thing we can control: our response to it.

When we react poorly to a difficult event in our lives, we give it more power over us. It is normal to feel upset, exhausted, and frustrated, but if we allow negativity to consume our thoughts, then we will only add to the amount of mental clutter that the event creates. If we can learn to change our reactions to situations and reframe them in our minds, we can change their impact on our minds. Here are some methods you can use to prevent the buildup of mental clutter and respond to tough situations in more constructive ways.

Start Journaling

If we have trouble dealing with and expressing our emotions, they can build up inside of us. We might try to quietly manage them without letting anyone else know how we feel, or we might try to communicate our feelings but lack the ability to put them into words. Either of these two options leaves us with tons of clutter since the thoughts we can't express build up in our minds and ensure that we are never over difficult events we experience.

A journal is a great way to take all of the clutter in our minds and put it somewhere else. When we write out our thoughts, we transfer them from our minds to the page. Rather than allowing our thoughts to spiral in our heads, we find a way to express them that reduces the burden in our brains while still allowing us to deal with problems privately if we so choose.

Additionally, journaling can help you process everything you're feeling. When your emotions only exist in your head, it can be tough to identify exactly how you feel and why you feel that way. When you get into the habit of writing these thoughts down, you become better at detangling your feelings from one another and uncovering the reason behind each strong emotion. This can help you decide how you should deal with the situation, and it usually provides results much faster than turning the same thoughts over in your head again and again throughout the day.

Writing things down is a great exercise for mental decluttering even outside of journaling. It follows the same idea, which is that getting things down on paper frees up space in our heads. Write down grocery lists, keep a calendar for important dates, and jot down the last episode you watched of the TV show you're currently binging. All of these things add unnecessary clutter to your mind and pull your focus away from the things that are actually worth memorizing.

Practice Thought Exercises

As mentioned previously, meditating isn't enough to completely rid your mind of clutter. That's still true, but it's also true that meditating and similar thought exercises can be a part of your decluttering journey. Meditation isn't just for people who love yoga. It can be a powerful tool for calming your thoughts when they get to be too much to handle. When practiced routinely, meditation can help you settle your mind and reorganize your thoughts, helping you assess any problems from a calmer vantage point.

Another thought exercise that can help you reduce clutter is mindfulness. Like journaling, mindfulness is especially useful for managing out-of-control emotions. Practicing mindfulness means that you shift your focus away from the past and the future and only focus on the present moment. Instead of worrying about everything that went wrong yesterday or that could go wrong tomorrow, you only consider how you feel right now. How does the current situation make you feel, and why do you feel that way? If you feel angry, distraught, or worried, that is okay since another big part of mindfulness is not blaming or judging yourself for negative feelings. Accept how you feel, take the time to process it, and then let the worst of these feelings go once you have come to terms with them. They will no longer take up nearly as much space in your mind. The chaos brought about by worrying about your future and past will subside as you start recentering your thoughts on the present moment and improving your ability to focus.

Ensure You're Getting Good Sleep

Exhaustion makes it harder for us to deal with difficulties in our lives. If we're tired, we're much more likely to snap at someone for a minor annoyance. We may turn a relatively minor event into a major crisis, if only in our perception of the event. Exhaustion can also interfere with our ability to learn, retain, and react to new information. We won't be able to put any of our decluttering strategies to use if we're not getting proper rest at night.

A busy schedule can sometimes make it hard to get the full eight hours that are recommended for adults. We might end up working late into the night or rising bright and early in the morning. We might be kept awake by buzzing energy because we had no opportunity to calm ourselves down after the business of the day. Cluttered thoughts might chase each other in our heads all night, leaving us lying awake and staring up at the ceiling as the clock ticks on. Reducing clutter in our lives can help us get the rest we need to reduce clutter in our heads.

Other strategies for combating insomnia include setting and sticking to a routine sleep schedule, avoiding activities right before bed, and doing something calming like gentle stretches or reading prior to laying down. Set aside dedicated time for relaxation so that you wake feeling refreshed rather than exhausted.

Talk to Loved Ones

Journaling and practicing mindfulness are good strategies for dealing with your emotions on your own, but sometimes, we need help from others. We aren't built to carry the weight of our burdens on our own. We are social creatures, and we need to feel connected to others in order to truly thrive. Our friends and families can provide support for us when we are going through a difficult time in our lives or if we just need to vent for a while. This is another way to transfer the clutter away from our minds. This time, by explaining how we are feeling out loud, we release the clutter into the air like we're shaking out a dusty rug. Through this process, we see that there are people in our lives who want to help us and who want to see us enjoying our lives rather than letting clutter take over.

Finally, discussing your problems with others can sometimes mean that they are able to help you find a solution. Maybe they cannot solve the problem entirely, but a friend or family member may be able to help you shoulder a responsibility until you can declutter your schedule, support you as you deal with a difficult life event, or provide assistance decluttering another part of your life. It's not always easy to open up to others, but when you do, you are often able to better manage your mental clutter.

Stick to the Essentials

If you were to look at all of the things you do in an average day and sort them into columns based on whether or not they were essential, how would you sort them? What would be essential, and what could be tossed aside? Try to identify the things that are most important to living a life that's fulfilling, not just a life that is comfortable. Next, make another list based on what's most important in the current moment.

Now, think about all of the things that you do that aren't essential to your well-being and happiness. What kinds of tasks are these? Are there any you can let go of completely, or will you have to replace them with more essential versions of those tasks? Where you can, try to eliminate the most unnecessary sources of mental clutter in your life. Look for responsibilities and habits that take more out of you than you get in return for doing them. Consider what kind of reward you get from completing each task, and if it's not something that you find valuable, see if you can find ways to drop it from your schedule.

After dropping the "dead weight" from your life, your thoughts should only be concerned with things that are important, primarily things that are important right now. Eliminating all of the unnecessary sources of stress in your life will help you reduce the rate at which mental clutter piles up. Unnecessary worries are removed from your mind, and you are free to focus on only things that matter.

Often, unnecessary tasks come from responsibilities we take on not for our sake but for the sake of others, even when we are already incredibly stressed and busy. They can also come from lifestyle choices that don't bring us any benefit but instead waste our time and energy. In order to truly free

our minds of clutter, we must get better at managing our daily schedules and deciding what is important enough to include in them.

Chapter Takeaways

In this chapter, we took a look at how our brains become cluttered and what we can do to reduce the clutter. We learned:

- Our brains are great at adaptation, but sometimes, their plasticity can work against us and increase our stress levels.

- We are predisposed to think negatively because we tend to take more notice of negative events than positive ones.

- We can declutter our brains by taking steps like venting our thoughts, using meditation and other mental exercises, improving our sleeping habits, and reducing clutter in our lives.

Now that we've taken a look at the ways clutter can manifest mentally, let's see what it looks like when it appears in your responsibilities.

Chapter 5: Decluttering Your Life and Responsibilities

"Don't count the things you do, do the things that count."—Zig Ziglar

Keeping busy is one thing, but packing our schedules full of unnecessary appointments, jobs, and other responsibilities is another. We need to stay active, but we don't need to fill our days with busywork that won't help us achieve important goals. If we accept too many responsibilities, especially ones that don't benefit us, we end up exhausting ourselves and ultimately missing out on the opportunities that would make a big difference in our lives.

Excessive responsibilities are a huge source of clutter in our lives. The problem may start innocently enough. Maybe we choose to take on some extra work at our jobs, not thinking much about the extra hour we're now spending working. Maybe we agree to do a favor for a friend that starts as a one-time offer and evolves into a recurring event. Perhaps we feel bad about taking time to relax while we have so many things on our plates, so we decide to combine our relaxation time with work in some way. Each of these situations is a trap that is surprisingly easy for us to fall into. Before we know it, they evolve into either a few time-demanding tasks or many tiny, insignificant tasks that waste a lot of effort when they are added together. The presence of any useless tasks in our schedules leaves us exhausted at the end of each day, and as we repeat the process for months or years at a time, we only grow more and more tired. We start to feel burned out all of the time, and thoughts of everything we have to do only pile on the anxiety and stress. A cluttered schedule is a guaranteed pathway to a cluttered mind.

One of the biggest problems that contribute to a cluttered lifestyle is when we prioritize simply being busy over making a positive impact on our lives. You've probably been given busywork at one point or another in your life, whether it was assigned by a teacher who didn't have a lesson planned for the day or a boss who didn't know how to maximize employee efficiency. If you've ever held a job in the service industry, you have probably been told you should try to look busy at all times regardless of whether or not the task you occupy yourself with is necessary. The reinforcement of these kinds of ideas worms its way into our heads until we are convinced that trying to do as many things as possible is the best way to work. But is this true?

Think of the phrase, "Work smarter, not harder." If you can accomplish a task just as well in a shorter time, or if the task in question is only wasting your time without providing significant benefits, you are better off taking the more efficient path. In fact, many studies have shown that when we follow the advice of the old phrase, giving ourselves time to rest in between periods of work, we accomplish more. We are able to focus on the tasks that are more important instead of wasting our time on things that merely keep us occupied. One study that examined employees who were assigned busywork even found that "unnecessary work tasks were prospectively associated with a decreased level of mental health" (Madsen et al., 2014, para. 3). These tasks drain our energy and our enthusiasm. Worse, they subtly convince us that our efforts don't matter. This mindset extends far past the unnecessary tasks until we start believing that even the critical tasks are as unimportant as the rest. What we end up with is a confused sense of which responsibilities are important, little to no downtime, and an incredibly cluttered mind.

Decluttering our schedules can be a complicated process since it's not always easy to tell which tasks are important and which aren't. We may be tempted to decide certain activities are important merely because we have been doing them for a long time, and we don't want to think of that time as wasted effort. We might assume a task is useful, but when we sit down and think about whether or not it has helped us throughout the years, we see that it has had little effect on our level of success. It's not always easy to accept that we're burning energy on things that don't matter, but if we choose to leap to being defensive, we will only continue to waste this energy. By intervening and putting a stop to these tasks when we can, we reduce the amount of clutter in our schedules, thereby significantly reducing the clutter in our minds.

There are two main problems to address when decluttering our schedules. The first is the issue of multitasking, which is a much bigger detriment than we may initially believe. The second is a lack of prioritization. If we can learn to leave multitasking behind and start prioritizing the tasks that matter, ditching all the rest, we can significantly limit how hectic and cluttered our lives are.

The Trouble With Multitasking

Multitasking was once a very popular recommendation for people who had busy schedules. Instead of doing just one task at a time, you could do two or even three. Surely this would save a lot of time in the long run, or at least, that was what people believed. Recently, multitasking has started to fall out of fashion as the flaws in the system have been exposed. More and more often, suggestions on how to free up more time in your schedule include "eliminate multitasking," even if these same people were espousing the glory of multitasking only a few years ago. What happened to change the public perception of multitasking? Is it as bad as some people say it is, and if so, why?

Theoretically, multitasking should let you get work done faster. Perhaps in some situations, it does. You might be able to perform small tasks that don't require a lot of your concentration at the same time. For example, you could wash dishes and watch an episode of a TV show, and you probably wouldn't miss much from either task. However, problems arise when you try to combine two intricate tasks or if you are trying to complete two tasks with very different goals in mind.

First, let's start with the latter of the two problems. If your main goal is washing the dishes and you merely turn on the TV to keep you company as you wash, you probably won't have any issues. You might miss a line here or there, but if you're not that invested in what's happening, it's no big deal. You might wash dishes a little slower if you pause to watch something, but if you're not trying to finish the task quickly, this isn't such an issue either. However, if you are trying to use TV time as a way to relax, adding a task like washing dishes into the mix could take away the value you would otherwise receive. Now, you're not fully relaxing; you're working. Instead of completing two tasks at the same time, you've effectively rendered one of the tasks worthless.

This might be a reason why you think you're getting enough free time in your day when you're really not. If you tend to interrupt your free time with small busywork tasks, you diminish the relaxing aspect, which means you never rest.

Now, we'll take a look at what happens if you're trying to do two complex tasks that both demand your attention. If you try to deal with both things at once, your brain is going to get confused. We're not built to flip between tasks rapidly, and we're not built to keep two different things in our minds at the same time.

Imagine you're a student trying to finish your math and history homework at the same time. If you complete a few math problems, switch to your history essay, and then switch back, your brain has to shift modes each time. It's not easy to remember your multiplication tables when you're wrapped up in historical dates. You could confuse the two, or it might take you some "processing time" each time you switch tasks. You will lose your train of thought as ideas for one topic intrude upon the other. You will likely end up taking much longer to complete the work than you would have if you'd just finished your math before you moved on to history. The danger of compulsive multitasking is that we don't realize that we're wasting time by working this way. We believe we're saving time when, in reality, all we're doing is splitting our attention, decreasing the quality of our work, and confusing ourselves.

Splitting Your Attention

You've probably heard the phrase "in the zone" before. It refers to a state of mind where you are completely focused on the task at hand. Ideas come easily, and you operate at a near-expert level. If you're exercising, you move faster and more confidently than ever before. If you're typing something, your fingers fly across the keys without hesitation. If you're reading, you finish a chapter in a matter of minutes, completely engrossed in the text. In each of these examples, a heightened ability is a direct result of remaining focused on one task without any distractions.

If being "in the zone" and focusing exclusively on one task is the height of productivity, then anything that distracts you from your current task must get in the way of your focus. Trying to multitask divides your attention between two or more tasks, effectively resulting in neither of them getting the attention they need to be completed efficiently. Without focus, you spend much longer on each task than it would otherwise require. This only adds to an already busy schedule. Instead of cutting your work in half, you may have inadvertently increased it simply because you've made it impossible to focus.

This lack of focus adds additional clutter to your mind because your brain tries to jump between different topics. When you don't let your thoughts settle into one activity at a time, thoughts of both tasks take up space, doubling the amount of mental clutter you experience. Without proper focus, overthinking takes control. This is just another of the many ways in which multitasking adds more work to your schedule, ultimately adding more clutter.

Declining Work Quality

The more we try to do at once, the harder it is to maintain high standards for our work. When we split our focus, the quality of our work may suffer as a result. Additionally, having a packed schedule already has us feeling rushed to complete each task on our to-do list. This can lead to mistakes and poor quality as well. As our work quality suffers, we may start to doubt our ability to produce great work, even if we aren't multitasking or rushing. This is fueled, in part, by the negativity bias. We tend to only see the times we have fallen short in our work or responsibilities and not the times where we have succeeded. We start to believe that our average work quality is the same as the kind of work we produce when we are under pressure. This can all culminate in a lot of self-doubt about our abilities.

Self-doubt only adds to the amount of clutter in our lives. Feelings of inadequacy, low self-esteem, and uncertainty generate a lot of mental clutter. Our minds buzz with activity, reminding us that we've fallen short and making us believe that we will continue to do so. Negative thoughts abound, and it becomes hard to calm our minds.

Are You Trying to Do Too Many Things at Once?

Self-esteem issues, exhaustion, and a lack of focus are all products of trying to do too much at once. When we multitask to the point that we overwhelm ourselves, we end up far more tired than we would be if we just took tasks one at a time. By trying to complete many different tasks at the same time, we only succeed in filling our minds with extra noise.

Of course, this desire to multitask stems from having an incredibly busy schedule in the first place. When we are constantly working on one task or another, we feel the urge to try to get them done faster, unknowingly accomplishing the exact opposite. While no longer multitasking can help us free up some time in our schedules, it doesn't take away any tasks. We are left with the same amount of work. If we don't make significant changes to the way we approach work, including cutting down on the sheer number of tasks and only doing activities that provide value, we will always be stuck in the same mentality that caused us to multitask in the first place.

How to Prioritize What Really Matters

We want to feel like everything we're doing is worth the time and effort we spend on it, but often, this just isn't true. Sometimes, we do certain tasks for very little reward or a reward that isn't proportional to the amount of time we spend on the task. If the task in question doesn't matter to us, we need to ask ourselves why we're doing it and whether or not it is worth continuing to do. Eliminating the unnecessary tasks from our schedules allows us to spend more time doing things that benefit us. We waste less time, and we provide ourselves with ample time for rest.

The most effective way to reduce clutter in your schedule is to learn how to prioritize your tasks. Ideally, every task on your to-do list should be ordered by its priority. This means that tasks that are very low priority may not get completed each day, or you may end up removing them from your schedule altogether. This is much better than having important tasks get pushed aside and put off even when you know you need to complete them. When you pare down your schedule to the bare essentials, performing only those tasks that help you feel fulfilled and accomplished at the end of the day instead of run-down, you make a lot more of the limited amount of time you have available to you each day. You can start taking on bigger projects that may provide more of a reward, and you can drop anything that isn't helping you be your best self. Prioritizing helps you declutter your schedule and lighten your workload every day.

Identify Your Core Values

What things matter the most to you in your life? If you had nothing at all, what would you most desire? If you had every possession you could ever want, what would you still look for in your life in order to make it fulfilling? The beliefs, values, and traits that are most important to you make up your core values. They represent the things that you can't live without and the things that you should always strive to achieve.

However, sometimes our lives don't line up with our core values. We waste time on things that don't hold any personal value for us, cluttering our lives with busywork and never feeling like we are making any progress on our goals. This is a reductive way to live that gets in the way of our growth and ability to feel fulfilled.

One exercise that can help you identify your core values is visualizing your dream life. Think about what your life would look like if you could make it anything you wanted. What kind of job would you have? Would you be well-off financially, or would you be fine with a comfortable amount of wealth? What would your house look like, and where would you live? What about your family? Would you weigh work a little higher than your personal life, or do your family and other personal relationships come before all else? Try to answer these questions as you think about what each aspect of your ideal future would look like.

Once you know what you want to achieve and what really matters the most to you, you can start looking at ways to achieve this life for yourself or at least come as close as possible. Eventually, you will start to remove tasks from your schedule that don't fit your goals and keep only the ones that help you make progress toward your dream life. For now, it is enough to just identify the things that matter to you personally.

Look at the choices you made when you visualized your future. Where did you assign value? Did you prioritize your career and wealth, or did you immediately start thinking about your future family? What kind of person are you in your dream life? Are you determined, driven, courteous, kind, and motivated? Are you good at maintaining relationships and listening to others? Do you provide value to your community? When you think about your future house, what does the interior look like? Do you value having a lot of stuff with plenty of clutter, or do you value a lack of clutter and a minimalist lifestyle? These core values are what make you an individual. They reflect what you care about most. You owe it to yourself to shape your life in a way that prioritizes these values so you can live the life you've always wanted.

Determine If Your Responsibilities Align With These Values

Now that you know what your core values are, you can decide if the tasks you occupy your day with support your efforts to live up to these values. The responsibilities you take on should reflect what you care about most. If not, why do them? You are just expending time and energy on tasks that don't matter to you. When your schedule is already cluttered, these kinds of tasks create unnecessary stress and anxiety. Reducing their presence in your life can bring you greater peace of mind.

You might wonder: How do I know if a responsibility aligns with my core values? After all, it's not like the tasks we take on come with a specific label of what kind of values they promote. However, you can figure this out by thinking critically about both the type of task you're doing and its results.

First, consider the benefits of completing a task. What, if any, kinds of rewards do you get from it? Is there a financial incentive, like there might be with a job or a favor you get compensated for? Do you get access to something you wouldn't otherwise, or is it something you do so you can maintain a good relationship with someone? Could you replace the task with something less time consuming or more beneficial to you and still get the same reward? If the reward that comes from a given responsibility isn't worth the effort you put in, or if the rewards don't align with the things you value, the task may be a good candidate to strike off your list.

Next, consider the risks of not completing the task. You know what you stand to gain, but what do you have to lose if you stop doing the task? There are some responsibilities that you cannot afford to give up. For example, you may not be able to leave a job you hate without securing a new one because you wouldn't be able to support yourself without it. On the other hand, there are many responsibilities that aren't very important to you at all. If you could stop doing something right now and face no negative repercussions, it's probably not something you need to continue doing. Sometimes, you might face minor discomfort or a brief period of uncertainty when you stop a task, but it ultimately wouldn't make too many waves in your life. These kinds of responsibilities are good contenders for ones you can safely drop from your schedule too.

Finally, consider if a task provides you with any inherent rewards. Some tasks are beneficial because of the work itself rather than any sort of reward others give you for completing it. A task may help you cultivate a valuable trait like focus, discipline, or persistence. These are worth learning and practicing as a form of self-investment. You might also spend your time improving your skills by engaging in a creative hobby. Alternatively, you may simply do something because you enjoy doing it. Playing a game may not come with any concrete rewards, and there may be no consequences for no longer playing, but that doesn't mean you should drop all games from your schedule. If it brings you enjoyment, you are still benefiting from the task in some way, as long as you don't allow it to take up all of your time.

Responsibilities that fit into any of these categories are worth keeping around. If something doesn't give you rewards relevant to your goals, there are no consequences for dropping it, and you don't enjoy doing it, then stop doing it. All it is doing is adding clutter.

Eliminate Any Unnecessary Responsibilities

After determining which responsibilities are necessary and which are unnecessary, you can rid your schedule of all of the unnecessary responsibilities. You may be able to stop some of them right away, or you may need to make alternative arrangements. Either way, try to plan on stopping this unnecessary work within the next month or so when possible. As you start to drop responsibilities from your schedule, you will be able to enjoy free time once again. You will find it easier to relax without the burden of more work looming over your shoulder, and you will spend less of your day dealing with responsibilities you don't care about or benefit from.

The additional advantage of cutting down your responsibilities to only those that benefit you is that now, everything you do will help you achieve your goals. Before, so much of the clutter in your life was purposeless. It didn't help you get where you wanted to be in life. After throwing out all of the clutter, you are left with only the important things. These will help you accomplish your goals without wasting your time, helping you become a more goal-driven and successful person. This is the hidden power of decluttering your life. It's not just about what you throw away; it's also about what is left and how it reshapes your life.

Chapter Takeaways

This chapter took a look at how your lifestyle and how busy you are can negatively impact your level of mental clutter. Some of the things you learned include:

- A cluttered life where you give yourself no opportunity to rest leads to burnout and frustration.

- Multitasking may seem like a good idea, but it usually ends up adding to the amount of time you spend on tasks rather than helping them go by faster.

- Prioritizing your tasks and eliminating those that don't help you achieve your personal goals will allow you to live a less cluttered life.

In the next chapter, we'll look at how your relationships can put a similar strain on your mentality and what you can do to fix this problem.

Chapter 6: Decluttering Your Personal Life and Relationships

"Avoid popularity; it has many snares and no real benefit."—William Penn

When we think of staying busy, we tend to think of things like our jobs and other professional responsibilities. Of course, these are not the only things in our lives that place burdens on our time. Our relationships can also eat up a significant amount of time, whether that time is spent socializing or doing various favors for friends and family members. This contributes to having a busier schedule with no time for relaxation since we make plans with others irrespective of how much free time we have available. Just like when we crowd our lives with work and other tasks, we end up working ourselves to exhaustion, except this time, it is even harder to recognize this as work. We might continue to offer our time to our friends because we think it's the right thing to do, but if we are hurting ourselves, we aren't helping anyone, least of all the people in our lives who would want us to be happy.

Additionally, if we have too many people to keep up with in our personal lives, this can add to mental clutter. We end up spreading ourselves thin, sacrificing time that could be better spent elsewhere. We also offer more of our mental space as the number of friends and acquaintances we have grows. The more important dates we have to remember at any given time and the more time we devote to socializing, the more cluttered we make our lives and our minds, especially if we aren't particularly invested in these relationships.

We want to think of all of our relationships as valuable, but many of them only exist to add clutter to our lives. Of course, this is not true of all of our relationships. We may have very close relationships with friends and family we care about a lot. As long as these relationships remain positive for both parties, they are worth any additional effort we make to maintain these relationships. However, the problem comes when we take great pains to maintain relationships that aren't especially valuable to us. These could be people who we know as a friend of a friend or those who we are just barely acquaintances with, or they could be relationships that started positive but have since faded over time. They may even include relationships that have become toxic and detrimental to one or both parties over time. If you are putting in a lot of effort to keep up relationships with people you barely know, or if you feel that you are trapped in a toxic relationship that is generating strife and mental clutter, it's time to make a change in the way you approach relationships.

The Myth of Popularity

Many people strive to have relationships with as many people as possible. Rather than trying to build a close-knit group of good friends, they seek out dozens of casual acquaintances, never able to spend enough time with any one person to make the relationship more meaningful. If you find that this is something you do, consider why you might be doing it. Are you just trying to meet and engage with new people, or do you find that with every new person who enters your life, someone else falls by the wayside? Are you trying to form these relationships because you genuinely care about everyone you spend time with, or are you prioritizing quantity over quality in an attempt to chase popularity?

Unlike what we might have been led to believe in high school, popularity doesn't do us any favors. In fact, we have trouble dealing with too many people in our lives at once. Our brains aren't built to keep up with so many different relationships on a personal level. As originally proposed by anthropologist Robin Dunbar and popularized by Malcolm Gladwell's book *The Tipping Point*, the maximum number of relationships we can deal with at any given time is 150. This is the "'point beyond which members of any social group lose their ability to function effectively in social relationships" (Sugihto, 2016, para. 2). Once we start dividing our time even more than this, we lose track of many of the people in our lives, and our relationships become more distant. All of the extra noise just turns into clutter in our minds rather than becoming something meaningful.

Ideally, we should try to keep the number of relationships in our lives at no more than 150, although even less than that is better if we can manage it. This helps to ensure that we are forging relationships for the right reasons and alleviates the burden of trying to remain in contact with hundreds of people.

Dealing With Toxic Relationships

Sometimes, relationships drain us for reasons other than simply being too numerous. A toxic relationship is one that is full of conflict, unhealthy competition, and a lack of support. Our friends and families should empower us just as much as we return the favor, but when there is an imbalance in a relationship or one party actively seeks to harm the other, these relationships can turn toxic.

Toxic relationships can come from many different areas of our lives. Someone we once thought of as a friend may become someone who takes advantage of us, routinely puts us down, or keeps us from achieving our full potential. A relationship with a spouse or other partner could become an abusive one, either verbally or physically. We might have a toxic relationship with our coworkers or bosses where we feel overworked and underappreciated, especially if we are expected to do things outside of our job description. Even our family members can be sources of toxicity in our lives.

As much as we might love these people, toxic relationships are especially draining. They introduce a lot of stress into our lives and put much more pressure on us than we would otherwise experience. We might go out of our way to appease these people with little if any reciprocity on their end. We end up sacrificing our time for people who don't help us grow. We may turn our frustration at these relationships inward, or we may internalize the negative things said about us in toxic relationships. All of these are forms of mental clutter that distract and harm us. It's not always easy to let a toxic relationship go, even when we recognize it for what it is. But when we do, we declutter our minds and start the healing process.

How to Identify Toxic Relationships

Recognizing that you are in a toxic relationship is not always as easy as it might seem. Many people who experience all of the signs of a toxic relationship don't even think to consider the relationship in that way, or they might make excuses for other peoples' behaviors. Without recognizing the problem, it is impossible to fix it. You will only end up hurting yourself more if you blind yourself to the possibility that a relationship is more detrimental than it might seem on the surface. Learning to recognize the warning signs can help you identify these relationships before they can do further harm.

Some warning signs are more immediately apparent than others. Any relationship that involves physical abuse, the threat of violence, or harassment is not just toxic but also highly abusive. These kinds of relationships put your well-being in danger. You may be tempted to rationalize and excuse your abuse, but at the end of the day, there is no justification for physical violence in a relationship, especially if the violence is used to manipulate you. Recognizing the danger these kinds of relationships pose to you can give you the strength you need to remove yourself from them and keep yourself safe.

Other warning signs are far more insidious and difficult to notice. Some relationships may involve subtle but persistent demands on your time and energy, or the other person may try to undermine your happiness. While these relationships don't necessarily pose a physical threat to you, this doesn't mean they're harmless. Far from it, in fact; if you fail to recognize these relationships as abusive, you may remain in them for much longer than you would remain in a physically abusive one. A common red flag is simply a feeling of unhappiness when you spend time with the person. If someone is constantly demanding your time and making you unhappy, then they are introducing toxicity and clutter into your life. If you experience a negative shift in your mentality, self-esteem, or mental health, consider if your relationships are contributing to this problem.

One more thing to look out for is a significant change in how you spend your free time or how often you spend time with other people. If you find yourself withdrawing from positive relationships in favor of ones that make you feel stressed and overwhelmed, you may be experiencing manipulation. Toxic people may try to keep you away from those who would otherwise help you recognize how harmful the relationship is. You should also keep an eye out for significant shifts in your personality, as red flags may be raised "when you're not your individual self anymore and you're giving everything to your partner" (Ducharme, 2018, para. 15) rather than finding happiness on your own terms. If you don't feel like yourself anymore, you will likely feel more distressed and experience more mental clutter as a result.

How to Let Go of Toxic People

Now that you have a good idea of the kinds of people who are adding toxicity to your life, you can work on either trying to correct the toxicity or separating yourself from these people. First, determine whether or not the relationship can be repaired. When toxic traits come from trauma or mental health issues, you may be able to encourage the other person to seek professional help to work through these problems. This is a possibility, but don't feel like it's the only option, nor should you feel like you're responsible for a friend or partner's mental health. If they are unwilling to seek help, the abuse doesn't stop, or you are simply unable to continue having a relationship with a person who has hurt you in this way, you are well within your right to end the relationship. Don't harm yourself by forcing yourself to forgive and forget. If what happened was unforgivable, or if you give someone a second chance and they don't improve, put your health first, and make the decision to leave.

Ending a toxic relationship can be difficult and sometimes dangerous, especially if there has been physical abuse or threats of violence. If you are worried about your safety and afraid to leave because of the risk of retribution, you may need to get the authorities involved. Even if you choose not to press charges against an abuser, contacting professionals in the domestic violence prevention field or in Child Protective Services can provide you with valuable resources and keep you safe as you separate yourself from a toxic household.

Of course, letting go of toxic people in your life can be difficult even if there is no physical abuse involved. There may still be mental and emotional manipulation that makes you reluctant to leave. Keep an eye out for relationships where you've given three, four, five, or more chances—these people aren't likely to change, and every time you give them another chance, your mental health suffers. If you find it intimidating to leave these relationships through your own willpower, rely on the support of genuine friends and family members who you have a positive relationship with. These people care about you, and they can help you break off the relationship in a way that prioritizes your safety and happiness.

Forming Healthy Relationships

It's hard for many people who have been in toxic relationships for a long time to form healthy relationships instead. We may always feel like we're waiting for the other shoe to drop, which interferes with our ability to communicate and relax around others. We may unknowingly engage in new toxic relationships instead of replacing them with healthy ones. To defeat the mental clutter caused by unhealthy relationships, we must create a social circle full of loving, supportive people who are understanding of our needs and desires. It is only through forging these positive relationships that we can start to undo some of the damage of the old, negative ones.

Communication is a key part of any healthy relationship. If we can't communicate with our family, friends, and partners, we will bottle our emotions up inside and fill our heads with emotional clutter we can't express. We should strive to be open and honest in our relationships whenever possible. This doesn't mean that you have to immediately discuss past trauma or other sensitive personal information with near-strangers; you should only talk about these things when you feel comfortable. But if you find that you are holding yourself back out of fear of punishment or having this information manipulated and used against you, stop and consider if this gut reaction makes sense. Do you think this person would do that based on their past behaviors, or are you projecting your old friend or partner's behaviors onto them? Try to rationalize these thoughts when you notice them. If you need personal space, be honest about this too. People who care about your well-being will understand, and they will be there to support you when you are ready to let them in.

Healthy relationships also require boundaries. It's not fair to either party if one person is constantly demanding the time and attention of the other. It's also not healthy to allow friends to cross lines you're not comfortable with. First, determine what your boundaries are. Figure out what you're okay with and what you're not okay with. It's okay if some of your boundaries are a little stricter than others if you feel you need them to be right now. Then, take the most important step: Communicate your boundaries to the people in your life. Make sure they understand what's acceptable behavior and what's not, and listen to what their boundaries are in return. Once you've explained your boundaries to the other person, they have no excuse for crossing them. If you know they are aware of the boundaries but continue to demand your time, take up your energy, and trivialize your desires, these should be huge red flags. Anyone who repeatedly doesn't respect your boundaries is not a good candidate for a healthy relationship. Walk away from these toxic relationships before they can get any worse.

If you struggle with honesty or boundaries because of past negative experiences, you may find it helpful to talk to a mental health professional. Speaking to a therapist, counselor, or psychologist can give you a better understanding of what you experienced and the ways it affects your behavior. They can also provide you with helpful coping strategies you can use to clear your head of harmful, spiraling thoughts.

Once you've established the basic foundations of healthy relationships, you can begin expanding these relationships past the surface level.

Building Deeper Relationships

We are heavily social creatures. The number and quality of our relationships impact all areas of our physical and mental health. If we withdraw from relationships entirely, we harm ourselves. If our relationships are all very shallow and we don't make any deeper connections, we don't benefit much more than if we had no relationships at all. Research has found that "good relationships help people live longer, deal with stress better, have healthier habits," and may even offer "improved lifespans" (Brickel, n.d., para. 3). Deep, supportive relationships reduce mental clutter and improve our lives, so they are more than worth investing in.

Not all of your relationships need to be deep. You can have some casual friends and acquaintances, but you should have at least a few people you can be completely honest and genuine with and who you can always rely on to help you out of a dark place. You can identify good candidates for these roles by considering who motivates you to become a better person just by being around them and who you naturally enjoy spending time with. Look for people who make any task fun just because you're in their company. Invest in people who build you up. Take an active role in the friendship to encourage its development. This means reaching out when you haven't seen each other in a while, making plans, and being emotionally available. If you focus your energy on the relationships that matter instead of those that are purely superficial or toxic, you will get the social support you need without all of the mental clutter.

Most importantly, remember that you deserve to be happy. You deserve relationships that make you feel good about yourself. You deserve people in your life who will support you and who want you to succeed. When you devote time or mental energy to spending time with someone who genuinely cares about you and who you care about in return, it won't feel like a sacrifice, and it won't add clutter to your life. It will be a source of stress relief rather than a source of stress. As you forge more of these healthy, positive relationships, your mental clutter will decrease significantly, and you'll feel so much better about yourself and your life.

Chapter Takeaways

In this chapter, we took a look at our social lives and discussed ways we can remove the more stressful aspects. You learned:

- Overextending yourself and trying to keep up too many relationships at a time is exhausting and adds to mental clutter.

- Removing toxic people from your life can get you all of the benefits of a good relationship without any of the stress of the unhealthy ones.

- Making new, healthy relationships and forming meaningful connections with others helps you push back against clutter from previous negative experiences and stay motivated through all of the ups and downs of life.

In the following chapter, we will discuss ways to declutter your home just like you've decluttered your schedule and relationships.

Chapter 7: Decluttering Your Home

"Instead of thinking I am losing something when I clear clutter, I dwell on what I might gain."—Lisa J. Shultz

Clutter in the home is almost omnipresent. Every time we turn a corner, we're all but assaulted with visual information. Trying to retrieve something from a cluttered closet turns a five-second activity into a half-hour excursion, if you even end up finding what you're looking for. It's frustrating, it wastes our time, and it makes it impossible to truly relax, especially if we want to clean up but never seem to get around to it. This is the last thing you want your home to be. The home should be a space for relaxation, but instead, it becomes a place just as chaotic and hectic as much of the outside world.

Clutter isn't just bad because it's unappealing or because you're more likely to lose something. It has a real, measurable impact on our minds and our ability to focus. Minimalists routinely preach about the dangers of living in a messy environment, and their arguments are backed up by science. In a 2011 experiment, "neuroscience researchers using fMRI (functional magnetic resonance imaging) and other physiological measurements found clearing clutter from the home and work environment resulted in a better ability to focus and process information, as well as increased productivity" (Sander, 2019, para. 10). If our living spaces are cluttered, we lose our ability to maintain focus. Our minds jump from one thing to another, and our thoughts become endlessly restless. Physical clutter in the house is also referred to as visual noise. Just like regular noise, the louder the visual noise is in an environment, the harder we find it to work, let alone to relax.

The good news is that reducing clutter in your home doesn't have to be a painful process. You can apply the basic concepts of minimalism to sort through your belongings, keeping those that provide value and getting rid of those that don't. It's not always easy to agree to let go of things that you've been keeping around for years, especially if you tend to be a bit of a pack rat, but if you can learn to reject the superficial trappings of an overly material world, you will find that decluttering your home follows naturally.

Making Your Living Space Livable

Cleaning out your living space can feel like a mountain of a task, but it's much simpler than it might seem. You just need to use a few tricks to your advantage. The first is to be more aware of how you interact with your environment. Pay attention to what you use, and more importantly, pay attention to what you don't use. You can even start marking things or otherwise flagging them when they get used. If you look back on everything you've flagged over a week, the things you left untouched are probably good candidates for things you can get rid of. If you extend this experiment to a month, are there any non-seasonal items you still haven't used? Chances are that if you haven't used them within a month, you probably don't need them as much as you think you do.

Another good tip is breaking the work down into more manageable chunks. Decluttering your whole house is going to sound like way too much work. You couldn't possibly do it all in one day or even one week. You see it as such a colossal task that you subconsciously start to push it to the back of your mind. Before you know it, months have gone by, and you've made no decluttering progress. Instead of worrying about the whole house, start by focusing on a single room. You can even begin with just one area of a room, like your bedroom closet or your kitchen pantry. Start with something easy to get into the rhythm of decluttering. Then you can expand your radius, steadily progressing through each room. When you break the work up into smaller pieces, it is suddenly a much more manageable task.

Finally, having a good routine for how you declutter will save you a lot of time spent hemming and hawing over what really matters and what really doesn't. Develop a system for figuring out if something should stay or go, and follow the same system for every room you declutter. As you practice the habit, it will get easier to get rid of the unnecessary things every time. You can use the following four-step method for effective decluttering every time.

Judge the Worth of Your Possessions

The first step to decluttering any space is figuring out what's clutter and what's not. You don't need to empty a room to declutter it. You only need to get rid of the things that you don't use and that don't provide any value. To do that, you have to learn how to assign value to your possessions.

One reliable way to decide if something is still worth keeping around or not is to consider when you last used it. Chances are that if it's been months or years since you touched something, you probably don't need it. Whatever emergency you're keeping it around for isn't nearly as likely to happen as you think. If something has been sitting under your bed or at the back of a closet for multiple years, it's not providing any value. Think of your home as an apartment building with you as the landlord and your items as your tenants. Your tenants have to pay 'rent,' which is a measure of how useful they are. If a tenant fails to pay rent for multiple months in a row, landlords generally kick them out because they're not holding up their end of the bargain. Don't let junk stay in your house rent-free either.

Be sure to check any items that have expiration dates when you're decluttering. This includes food, medications, makeup, personal hygiene products, and cleaning products. All of these things can go bad if you don't use them up in time. Chances are that if you let something expire, you probably had little intention of using it in the first place, or it didn't live up to your initial expectations. Toss anything that's expired automatically, and try to avoid purchasing it again in the future. Alternatively, if it's something you use only occasionally, try to buy a smaller size so less goes to waste.

There are some valid reasons to keep things around even if they're not constantly in use. Some items may not be used frequently, but they still serve a purpose. For example, just because you haven't set the kitchen on fire yet doesn't mean you should throw the fire extinguisher out. Still, you should probably check to make sure your fire extinguisher has been serviced recently so that it still functions. Keep similar items only for as long as they are good for, then replace them when necessary. A good rule is to use common sense when decluttering. Don't throw out things that could keep you safe in a dangerous situation; focus on the things with little to no purpose that pose no threat to you if you were to remove them.

Another reason you might want to keep something that gets little to no use is sentimental value. It is okay to keep things around because they are personally meaningful, but be careful when applying this label, and try to keep the number of purely sentimental items in your home as low as possible. More often than not, we claim something is sentimental as an excuse to keep it around, not because it is. Be honest about how much an item means to you. If you would be devastated to see it go, then it's okay to keep; otherwise, it's probably not particularly sentimental.

Ask these questions about each item you come across in your cleaning process. Decide if the item serves a purpose, if that purpose is useful, and what that purpose is. If something doesn't meet these criteria, it's not valuable after all.

Sort Everything Into Piles by Usefulness

Now that you know how valuable everything is, you can figure out whether or not you should keep it. Separate the things you deemed useful from the things you decided served little if any purpose. You can technically do this by making a list, but I prefer to do it by physically sorting the items. Clear space for three distinct piles. The first pile is for the things you're definitely keeping. The next is for the things you might or might not keep. The final pile is for everything you've decided doesn't add value to your life.

Let's start with the first pile, which includes everything that you're confident about keeping. Try to keep this pile as small as possible. Reserve it for only those items that serve a significant purpose and get plenty of use. This pile should be primarily everyday items that you use at least once a week on average. It can also include a few important items that still see occasional use.

We'll skip the second pile for now and look at the pile full of things you want to get rid of. These are the items you've decided hold little value, the things you bought impulsively, or the things that have worn out their welcome. They will probably be a mix of things that are well-worn and things that are completely pristine. This is perfectly normal. Sometimes, we don't use the things we buy, even if we thought we would when we bought them. We might be tempted to keep these things just because we feel like we didn't get our money's worth out of them, but this doesn't do us any favors. We're better off reducing the clutter and tossing these items when they no longer have worth for us. In the next step, we'll take a look at ways we can repurpose or gift these items so that they're still serving a purpose for someone else.

If you can't decide whether to sort something into the first or third pile, put it in the second. This is the pile for anything you're not sure about keeping. If you're trying to decide how often you use something, leave it in this pile for a bit. Transfer these items to a bin or another container so that they're out of the way but also easily accessible. You can leave them here for about a week, depending on the kinds of items and the frequency at which they would normally be used. If you need to use an item, take it out of the bin and use it, but don't put it back in the bin. Instead, return it to its original location. After a week or so, look back at the bin. The items that are still there are those that you never used. At this point, you can pretty safely label these items as ones to be tossed.

Toss, Donate, or Keep

You've got your piles, and you know what you're doing with each one. Take all the things you've decided to keep and set them off to the side. We'll come back to this pile in the next step. For now, we want to focus on the things we're getting rid of.

You've probably realized by now that if you were to just throw out all of the clutter in your house, you'd generate a lot of garbage. On top of that, you would be throwing away a lot of things that aren't necessarily ready for the trash. Just because something isn't useful to us doesn't mean it's not useful to anyone. We can do a lot of good by donating and gifting things that are still in good condition and may hold value for other people. This can encourage us to declutter too since we don't feel like we're just generating trash. We feel like we're having a positive impact on our community and making a difference, which inspires us to be more liberal with the things we decide to release from our lives.

First, look through your pile for anything that can be repurposed. These items might not hold much value in their original forms, but they can be recycled into something more beneficial. For example, a stray sock missing the other half of its pair could become an easy way to wipe dust off of surfaces. The jar from a used-up candle could become a storage container for small items or a pot for a tiny plant. Clothing that's well-worn and full of holes can be torn up further and turned into rags for cleaning. By transforming items in this way, you give them new value without being wasteful.

One word of caution on repurposing: Only keep something around with the intention to repurpose it if you are planning on using it soon. Try not to save these things for "a rainy day" since they often end up sitting and waiting to be used. This turns them back into clutter, which is the last thing you want to do. If you do keep things around to repurpose, don't put them back where they were before. Move them so they're grouped with other items that share their new purpose. This means that in the case of the stray sock, you should move it out of the sock drawer and store it with your cleaning supplies instead. This increases the chances you'll remember to use it. Keep only the things that you can repurpose and use in the near future, and disregard any DIY materials that are more likely to sit and gather dust.

Next, see if you can identify any items that would make good gifts for people in your life. Maybe you have a purse you like but rarely use anymore. If you think someone else would enjoy it, set it aside as a way to brighten their day sometime soon. Old books are great gifts too, especially if you know someone who would enjoy the story as much as you did.

Depending on the types of items you are left with, you may be able to donate them. Clothing and canned goods are some of the most commonly donated items, but they're far from the only ones. Most shelters are also in need of spare toiletries and personal hygiene products, and donating any unopened packages you have can be a big help. Pet shelters are often in need of spare towels and pillows, and they rarely care about the quality of the items. Some libraries will accept donations of books and other media like movies, CDs, and records. Some charities accept toys and sporting goods. Occasionally, you can donate furniture that is still in good shape to certain organizations. Check with local donation collection centers near you to see what they accept and what they're most in need of. Also, make sure to check the expiration dates on anything that you're planning to donate so that you don't end up sending expired goods.

Once you've exhausted all other options, use the trash as your last resort. This helps you minimize the amount of waste you create while still leaving you with a home free from clutter. While the trash is usually a good catch-all for items that can't be disposed of or repurposed in another way, watch out for items that shouldn't get thrown away. Some electronic devices, corrosive materials, and medications have specific disposal methods that you should follow. Additionally, recycle anything you can to avoid plastic and glass pollution.

At the end of this step, you will finally be free of the clutter that has taken over your living space for so long. From this new, clutter-free vantage point, the amount of storage space you have available may seem larger than ever before. All that's left is for you to return to the pile of items that you've decided to keep and organize everything that's left.

Organize What's Left

A good organization system helps prevent future clutter. If you know where everything is and everything has its place, you can find what you need quickly, and you're more likely to put it right back where you got it. Gone are the days of endlessly hunting around for that one thing you need in a huge pile of things you don't need. When you get organized, you'll save yourself time and hassle, and you'll also make it less likely that you'll fall back into your old habits.

The period right after a big clean-out is the perfect time to organize what you have. There is a lot more space available to you, so make good use of it! When you put things away, try to group them in ways that make sense and help you find what you're looking for easier. Instead of throwing books and movies haphazardly back on your shelf, organize them in alphabetical order. Rather than putting all of your clothes back in your closet, hang up the clothes that are currently in season, and store the rest until you're going to wear them again. Know where everything is, and pack away anything you're not currently using.

You also want to arrange each room in a way that looks tidy visually. Just because everything's organized doesn't mean it's not still visually loud. A library might follow the Dewey decimal system religiously, but most libraries aren't exactly minimalist. The best way to do this is to find storage solutions that are 'hidden' or otherwise out of sight. Make use of space under the bed, in drawers, and in closets, so long as you can keep these areas organized and the things inside them easily accessible. Put things away in storage bins, jars, baskets, and other containers to group similar items. This will give each room a clean, open look with minimal distractions.

Finally, move things where you tend to use them. It wouldn't make any sense to put your TV in one room and your remote control in the other, so why do we do this with so many other items? Keep toiletries in the bathroom, laundry supplies by the washing machine (or where you pile your dirty clothes if you use a laundromat), and video games near their consoles. If you want to read more, a neat trick is to take the book you're currently reading and store it not with your other books, but instead nearby wherever you're most likely to read it. For example, if you want to start reading before bedtime, leave the book on the nightstand by your bed. This way, it's easily accessible to you, which means you're more likely to read it. Rather than adding clutter, you improve your ability to focus on a task you might have otherwise put off or forgotten about.

What you're left with after all of this decluttering and reorganizing are the most important items.

You have gotten rid of the sources of distraction and visual noise that once dominated your house. Now that all of the hard work is done, you'll likely find it easier to relax, focus, and live in your newly decluttered home.

Preventing Future Clutter

You might be asking yourself: Didn't you just say the hard work is over? Actually, the hardest part is over. When you start with a neat, organized home you've just rid of many unnecessary items, it's not hard at all to keep it that way. Still, you don't want to go back to your old bad habits. If you don't make some changes in the way you treat your home and the things inside it, you might turn around in a few months to find that all of the clutter has somehow returned. Thankfully, there are two simple rules to follow to prevent clutter from coming back. The first is to adjust your spending habits, something that you'll want to do anyway to save yourself money. The second is to make cleaning and decluttering something you do routinely.

Stop Buying Things You Don't Need

Impulse purchases account for a lot of the clutter we generate over the years. When we don't think hard about what we're buying, we don't get a chance to decide whether or not the item is worth having around. We might use shopping as a pick-me-up when we're experiencing a hardship, which makes the tendency to spend money on unnecessary things even worse. The more we spend compulsively, the more clutter we accumulate over time, and we end up hardly touching half the things we buy.

We can train ourselves out of this behavior by stopping to consider the value of everything we buy. We might think that a pair of heels would be cute, but how often would we wear them? Maybe it's better to invest in a comfortable and cute pair of sneakers, which we would wear far more often. When we pause before making a purchase, we give ourselves time to analyze the value said purchase would bring to our lives. If it's not going to bring any value, it will only end up as clutter.

Make Decluttering Part of Your Routine

Here's a fun fact you might have heard before: The cells in your body are constantly growing, dividing, and dying. New cells are made as quickly as the old ones die off, and the lifespan of a cell is not nearly as long as that of a human. Because of this, it's estimated that the human body completely replaces all of its cells about every seven years (Opfer, n.d., para. 3). Of course, this process doesn't happen all at once. It would be incredibly difficult for your body to generate enough energy to replace all of its cells at the same time, and you'd probably stop being able to function during this process. Instead, your body makes these changes gradually over the seven years. A relatively small number of cells are replaced every day, which eventually culminates in a much larger effect.

This is the same way you should treat the decluttering process. Despite your best efforts, you might still make a few impulse purchases here and there that can reintroduce junk into your household. If you wait years at a time to declutter, you're going to have a lot of work ahead of you. Breaking it down room by room helps to ease the difficulty a bit, but there's still a lot to do if you let the problem get worse and worse until it gets out of hand. Instead of waiting until the clutter is almost unbearable, start turning decluttering into routine maintenance, which is much better for your mind and much easier on you. If you do a little bit of decluttering every few months, you can get the same amount of work done with much less energy expended. Even better, this helps you maintain a good standard for how cluttered you allow your house to be, which reduces the risk of developing mental clutter once again.

Ideally, you want decluttering to become something you do routinely. Try to set specific dates because this helps you hold yourself accountable for getting it done in a timely manner. Every two or three months, you should go around your house and get rid of any clutter that's built up over this time. You probably won't have to do much work. You might be able to get everything done in an afternoon, which is a lot faster than taking weeks to get rid of several years' worth of clutter. As long as you hold yourself to a high standard and address clutter when it initially appears, not when it's been given time to build up, keeping your home decluttered should be a breeze.

Chapter Takeaways

This chapter took a look at some of the reasons why a clutter-free home is necessary and supplied you with tips for decluttering your home. Some of these tips include:

- Be more mindful of how you interact with everything in your house, and pay attention to the things that rarely get used.

- Weigh the value of every item in your home. If it's not providing you any value, it's just taking up space.

- Don't give clutter problems the opportunity to get worse. Manage them early, and you'll save yourself a lot of work in the long run.

Next, we'll learn how to declutter what often feels like our home away from home: our workspaces.

Chapter 8: Decluttering Your Workspace

"Minimalism is not subtraction for the sake of subtraction. Minimalism is subtraction for the sake of focus."—Anonymous

Imagine you're working in a cubicle at an office. You have plenty of work to do but not so much that you can't goof off a little, you figure, and there are plenty of distractions on your desk that all seem more fun than your actual work. Maybe you waste a little time with these distractions, but you're ready to get back to work soon enough. But as soon as you do, one of your coworkers pulls your attention away again, pulling you into a discussion about some TV show or something equally trivial. Before you know it, an hour has gone by, and you haven't done any work at all. When you try to work, now keenly aware of how much time you've lost and how hard it has become to focus, your boss comes by and assigns you an additional project. Suddenly, it feels like your attention is being split a hundred different ways, and you can't keep up with everyone's requests. How can you possibly focus with all of this clutter?

As it turns out, you can't. The more distractions and diversions from your responsibilities that litter your workspace, the harder it becomes to focus on anything at all. Your mind fills up with unrelated, unimportant thoughts, and it becomes impossible to think clearly. This is especially bad if your job requires you to do a lot of critical thinking and problem-solving. Distracted thinking probably isn't going to get you great results, at least not compared to the results you would usually have. All of these distractions create clutter, and that's the last thing you want when you're trying to focus.

Decluttering your workspace is well worth the initial energy and time investment. It becomes much harder to locate important papers when you have a cluttered, disorganized desk or filing system. It's also much harder to put your head down and get your work done when dozens of things are vying for your attention at all times. Clutter leads to wasted time and diminished returns on the time you spend working. By decluttering your workspace, you reduce the risk of procrastination and become a more efficient worker.

Decluttering Your Desk

Whether you head into an office every day or work from home, you should have a dedicated workspace. At most jobs, this might mean a cubicle, a desk, or just an area where you're typically posted if you work a service or retail job. These kinds of spaces are specifically designed to improve workflow and sharpen your focus. Even if you share the area with your coworkers, you still get a space, whether it's a desk or another type of work area, that is exclusively for work. Of course, it's your responsibility to keep it this way, but we'll return to this in a moment.

If your home is your office, it's even more important to designate a specific area as your workspace. It's difficult to get into a working mentality if you're trying to do your work from your bed or your couch. Instead of focusing on your tasks and responsibilities, your thoughts will start to drift to the other things you usually do in the same area of your house. Additionally, your brain starts to make associations between where you are and what you do there. It's harder to turn on the work mindset if your brain is stuck in the relaxation mindset. This can make a tendency for procrastination worse. It also becomes hard to turn off the work mindset, which is an especially big problem if you try to work in your bed. This breaks down the association between your bed and sleeping, replacing it with working associations and making it harder to quiet your thoughts for long enough to fall asleep at night. The best way to remedy this issue is to set aside one part of your house as your home office. Get all of your work done there, and avoid bringing anything unrelated to work into that space.

Now that you have a specific area that you use for work, it's time to declutter it just like you decluttered your living space. Eliminate all possible sources of distraction, and try to keep only the things that help you complete your work. If you successfully keep your desk clear of distractions and time sinks, you'll find the amount of work you're able to complete each day will increase drastically.

Be Wary of Common Sources of Distraction

While anything can become a distraction in the right context, there are some items that are more effective at pulling our attention away from our work than others. These tend to be things that are more fun and interesting than our work. Our brains crave the little energy and mood boost we get from doing fun things, especially when we're working and craving something more enjoyable. Be on the lookout for anything in your workspace that isn't helping you get your work done, and try to remove these things before they can sabotage your progress.

Two of the biggest offenders are TV and video games. These are usually more of a problem for home offices, but your place of business might also have a TV set up. Games and TV are designed to hook us in. They're often meant to be pure fun, and we build up a lot of positive associations with them. This means that when we're offered a choice between work and play, we're going to pick play just about every time, regardless of whether or not we have the time to waste. The best way to deal with these distractions is to get them out of our sight when we need to buckle down and work. When we're not directly looking at something, it's easier for us to forget it's there. If you can, move the TV or video game console out of the room you're working in. If you can't, turning them off is your next best option. Just be sure to hide the remote or controller, ideally leaving it somewhere out of your reach. Sometimes, the simple barrier of having to get up to turn on the TV will remind you that you're not supposed to be watching TV right now. This brief pause is enough for your critical thinking skills to kick in and return your focus to your work. If your boss won't allow you to turn the TV off—for example, if you work in a doctor's office's reception area and the TV is on for patients—ask if you can at least mute the noise and turn on closed captions. This doesn't remove the problem entirely, but it will still drastically cut down on the amount of distraction the TV can create.

Not every distraction can be managed by simply getting it out of your sight. Sometimes, the source of distraction is part of your work. This is often the case with computers and cell phones. You might need your computer for your job, but it also gives you direct access to hundreds of distracting, clutter-inducing sites. With a few clicks, you can end up procrastinating hours of your time away. The same is true for your cell phone. You may be able to shut your phone off and leave it in your pocket or a bag in some situations, but dealing with the distraction becomes a lot harder when you need your phone for important work-related calls.

Luckily, as much as technology has the power to distract us, it has the power to help us reduce the risk of distraction too. There are many different software programs designed to help you be more productive, and a great deal of them work to eliminate the temptations that your phone and computer pose. You can install programs and extensions on your computer that will restrict your access to certain sites, some of which allow you to set a time limit and make it fairly difficult to bypass these restrictions. Similar apps exist for your phone that disable notifications for everything outside of calls and texts. This cuts down on the amount of buzzing your phone does every five minutes and ensures that every time you stop and check your phone, you're only looking at things relevant to work.

No matter what form distraction takes in your workplace, you can protect yourself from it by doing one of three things. You can remove yourself from the presence of the distracting thing if possible, you can move the distracting thing away from you so that you're not constantly reminded of it, or you can use creative solutions to diminish the risk of falling prey to distraction. Each of these solutions lets you keep your focus on your work so you can get it done.

Organize Your Workspace

Poor organization wastes your time. The longer you spend hunting down a file that's not where it's supposed to be, precariously balancing new clutter on top of all of the existing clutter on your desk, or combing through your emails looking for a specific one, the less time you have for work. As you eat away at your time, you end up having to rush through assignments to meet deadlines and expectations, which leaves you stressed and can bring self-critical thoughts to the surface. To avoid all of this, all you need to do is get organized.

Organizing your desk or another workspace isn't that different from organizing your home. You can follow the same basic principles of giving everything a dedicated home and returning things to this home after you've used them. This means you don't have to spend any time or mental energy trying to figure out where you left something; you'll always know right where it is. It's also a good idea to come up with a system for organizing new files or other resources. You can order them alphabetically, group them by their purpose, arrange them by their relevant dates, or use any other strategy that helps you find what you're looking for on the first try. Fruitlessly hunting for something is as frustrating as it is distracting, so the small amount of time you spend revamping your organizational system is worth the decrease in your mental clutter.

Finally, keep the surface of your desk clean. You might have to flip back and forth between different documents as you work, but as soon as you're done with them, you should return these files to their proper place in your organizational system. Try not to leave old drink bottles or food wrappers on your desk after you're done with them. Clear away sources of clutter like pens and pencils, keeping them in a cup or in a drawer instead. These are small changes, but they'll make a huge difference in keeping your workspace neat and organized.

Dealing With Clutter From Bosses and Coworkers

We tend to think of sources of distraction as inanimate objects, but people can be distracting too. As we discussed in the chapter about decluttering your relationships, other people can be a source of mental clutter. This is especially true at work, where too many conversations with coworkers or getting assigned too much work at the same time can make it significantly harder to focus our efforts where they're most needed. It's hard to get work done with someone always staring over our shoulder or even if they're just popping in and out, always seeming to appear at the most inconvenient times.

The worst thing about distraction that comes from our coworkers or bosses is that they often don't even realize they're adding to our mental clutter. A chatty coworker may just be trying to make friends at the office. A boss who tends to micromanage may honestly believe they're being helpful. This makes us reluctant to correct them because we don't want to hurt their feelings, but tolerating constant disruption and distraction isn't good for our mental health or our productivity. Again, as in all good relationships, honesty is key. Whenever the urge arises to sweep your concerns under the rug, counter it with an attempt to speak up for yourself. Otherwise, nothing's going to change.

Setting boundaries is equally important in the workplace. You need enough time to focus on your work if you want to get it done. When people interrupt you or make demands on the time you've set aside for yourself, they interfere with your ability to do your job. If you're a people pleaser, you'll probably be tempted to drop everything and give others your attention, but resist this urge. Instead, gently but firmly let them know you're busy and that you'll get back to them when you can. This isn't an unreasonable request, and most people will have no trouble granting it. If coworkers continue to bother you after you've made your boundaries clear, discuss the issue with your HR department, boss, or whoever is responsible for managing employee conflicts in your company. If your boss doesn't respect your boundaries and keeps adding to your mental clutter, it may be time to look for a new line of work. It's a tough decision to make, and you should give it a lot of thought, but you need to feel respected and valued in your job. If you're constantly overworked and overwhelmed by work-related stress, your job is creating too much mental clutter, and your talents may be better suited elsewhere.

Chapter Takeaways

In this chapter, we took a look at how your job can contribute to clutter and what you can do about it. We discussed many tips for managing workplace clutter, including:

- Remove distractions from your work environment to improve your focus.

- Create and stick to an organization system that you can navigate easily. This cuts down on wasted time.

- Set boundaries at work so you can concentrate on important tasks and get them done.

In the final chapter, we will learn how we can declutter not just the physical world but the digital world too.

Chapter 9: Decluttering Your Time Spent Online

"Your worth is not measured in likes, comments, notes, or followers, but in your ability to love, be kind and keep negative comments to yourself, take notes, and lead by example."—Mariah McHenry

Clutter in the digital world isn't always as easy to recognize as clutter in the physical world. You could certainly say that having multiple pages' worth of apps you don't use counts as clutter, but this is a minor annoyance at best. Digital clutter can be much more insidious and damaging than this, and it all has to do with the power technology has over us.

If you're an avid user of social media, the last thing you want to hear is how technology is bad for you. It can get exhausting to hear people talk about how everyone is so obsessed with their phones, to the point that you might roll your eyes whenever you hear the idea. After all, as you've probably said to yourself multiple times, technology is a great resource that connects us all to information at the touch of a button. Shouldn't we use this resource to our advantage?

While technology certainly has its positive uses, it also has the potential to be a source of negativity, overthinking, and mental health issues. Nowhere is this more apparent than on social media where the constant scramble for likes and followers and the need to constantly compare yourself to others can drive you to prioritize your digital persona over your real life.

Tech also poses the danger of getting you hooked, which can cause you to spend hours mindlessly scrolling and consuming meaningless content that clutters your brain. Websites and apps employ different motivation techniques to guarantee you keep returning to them, including "'scarcity' (a snap or status is only temporarily available, encouraging you to get online quickly); 'social proof' (20,000 users retweeted an article so you should go online and read it); 'personalization' (your news feed is designed to filter and display news based on your interest); and 'reciprocity' (invite more friends to get extra points, and once your friends are part of the network it becomes much more difficult for you or them to leave)" (Ali et al., 2018, para. 3). These are all incredibly effective ways to grab your attention and get you checking your phone every

10 minutes.

It's important to remember, however, that it's not the technology itself that is inherently dangerous; it's how we use it that poses a risk. If we declutter our digital spaces and reduce the risk of harm, we can maximize the positive results of technology and avoid all of the negative ones. When we consume digital content in reasonable amounts and don't allow it to take over our lives, we forge a much healthier relationship with technology.

Decluttering Your Feed

The people you follow and the posts you interact with on social media have a huge impact on what kind of experience you have with technology. As you know, the content you interact with on your social media accounts is different from the content your parents might interact with. Everyone is able to personalize their experience by following and unfollowing whoever they want. This is one of the most underutilized tools in the digital world. Curating your experience can help you avoid all of the worst parts of social media, including the toxic competitive nature, the endless negativity, and the subtle and persistent encouragement to always be online. By making changes to who you follow, you can vastly improve your experiences and cut down on clutter.

Unfollow Excessive Negativity

It's easy to get swept up in the more toxic, negative parts of the internet. A few complaints here and there won't give you much trouble, but certain people only ever seem to post about things that make us angry and upset. When we follow these people, we get a direct line to all of their negativity until we start to internalize it ourselves. Their frustration rubs off on us, and our mentalities suffer because of it. Worse, we may not even realize that we're doing this due to the whiplash-like nature of the tone of the posts on our feeds. A typical scroll through your timeline might include a joke, an incredibly negative post, and then another joke. The negativity flies past us so quickly that we hardly have time to recognize it, but our brains pick up on it thanks to our negativity bias. When we let depressing and aggravating posts sneak their way into our feeds on a regular basis, we allow this same negativity to invade our thoughts.

Luckily, you get to control the content on your timeline. You can decide whether or not you want to expose yourself to so much negativity. If you want to cut down on mental clutter and relieve social media-induced anxiety and overthinking, unfollow the people who repeatedly make you a more negative person. Sometimes, these will be strangers. Other times, you may need to unfollow someone you know in real life, even if you still enjoy their company in person. It's okay to unfollow anyone who is turning your feed into a cluttered, gloomy mess, and you shouldn't feel guilty no matter who it is. Prioritize your mental health first and foremost.

Limit Your Screen Time

The other big danger of most digital spaces is that they are designed to get us to keep scrolling. Most websites have implemented an auto-scroll feature, which means that instead of clicking a button to take you to the next page, posts simply appear when you hit the bottom of the current page. This is convenient, but it makes us more likely to continue consuming content. We feel like we have to like the next post or watch the next video that comes up. Auto-scroll eliminates the natural pauses in our attention that reaching the end of the page would have provided us, so we spend longer and longer on our phones and computers. If you struggle with excessive screen time, try setting a timer for 10 or 15 minutes when you open social media. Once the timer rings, put down your phone and move on to something else. This interrupts the endless flow of content and shows you just how long you're spending on social media. With this knowledge, you can decide if it's truly a good use of your time. You can also limit the time you spend scrolling by following fewer people. If there are fewer posts to read, you'll eventually run out of new content, which will force you to take a break.

You should also try to take breaks when you feel yourself getting excessively frustrated. Social media encourages interaction, but not all of that interaction is positive. You might get swept up into an argument or two, sometimes with a total stranger. While there's nothing wrong with having a discussion with someone on social media, when the discussion devolves into senseless arguing and bickering, it's time to take a break. It's not doing your mentality any favors to obsess over fights with strangers.

Stop Caving to FOMO

The fear of missing out (FOMO) is an incredibly strong motivator. We want to be a part of the action, and social media makes us feel like we're connected to others in the same position. This can give us a sense of community, but it can also be used to manipulate us into returning to the same website or app over and over again. Be wary of "limited time" offers and events because these prey on your FOMO and can lead to you spending far more time on the internet than usual. Look out for other ways that sites and content creators subtly influence your decisions, and pause to consider your actions instead of reacting impulsively. When you get a little perspective, it becomes a lot easier to recognize when someone's trying to manipulate you.

Decluttering Your Own Posts

It's not just other peoples' posts that we should be worried about. We can develop a toxic relationship with social media through our posts as well. This is especially dangerous when we start devoting more time and effort into our online presence than we do our real-life relationships. When we allow the digital world to start meaning more to us than the real world, we lose sight of the things that matter in our lives. We cave to our desires for instant gratification in the form of likes and comments, deeming them more important than our real experiences. All the while, thoughts of our posts crowd our heads. We keep thinking about posts that didn't do as well as others, wondering what we did wrong. We see the success of others, and we become jealous and frustrated. These emotions only make the clutter worse.

There is no 'winning' in the social media game. There is no amount of likes we can receive where we will feel truly happy about what we've accomplished. If all we care about is how many people click a button on our posts, then we will just keep chasing more and more likes, getting increasingly frustrated, and leveling criticisms at ourselves for something that's ultimately meaningless. The only way for us to break this cycle of negativity and clutter is to stop playing the game.

Limit How Often You Post

Just as you should limit the number of people you follow to avoid being overwhelmed with posts, so, too, should you limit the number of posts you make. Posting is addictive because it creates a positive feedback loop in your mind. As you start making more and more posts, possibly posting multiple times a day, you get more invested in the social media game. You start caring more about engagement and how well-received your posts are and less about whether or not they reflect an accurate picture of your life. As it turns out, many people who have picturesque lives on social media don't show the world their private struggles and hardships. You, too, can fall into this trap of pretending you have an ideal life instead of trying to achieve it.

Posting less frequently helps you keep your distance from this possibility. It keeps you from getting too wrapped up in the digital world and all of the clutter it creates. Enforce a hard post limit on yourself. If you usually post five or more times a day, cut it down to no more than twice per day. This way, you'll spend less time online and less time worrying about what people think of each post.

Chapter Takeaways

This chapter discussed the troubling and sometimes toxic relationships that are all too common with technology. You learned:

- The digital world, especially social media, is purposefully designed to be addictive and take up space in your thoughts.

- You can curate a more enjoyable and positive experience with social media by making changes to the ways you interact with technology.

- Improving your relationship with technology can reduce or even eliminate social media-induced mental clutter.

Conclusion

By now, you know just how harmful clutter can be. You know that it can bring you to the brink of exhaustion and cause you to become overly critical of yourself, getting in the way of your ability to grow and flourish. You also know that clutter isn't just the unread books you collect in your house or the old fast-food wrappers littering the interior of your car. It can arise from chaotic and hectic situations and experiences in all their forms. Your mind, lifestyle, friendships, home, job, and social media accounts can all be filled to the brim with clutter, ready to spill over into your life.

Even though clutter is a powerful force, you aren't powerless to stop it. In fact, you can take the steps necessary to rid your life of clutter in all of its forms. The most important takeaway from this book is that the power to shape your life is in your hands. If you allow clutter to persist, you're always going to be fighting a losing battle. You will make things harder for yourself in every area of your life you leave cluttered, and these difficulties will be reflected in your mental state.

If instead, you choose to sort through everything in your life, keeping the good and tossing out the junk, you'll find that these sources of resistance will disappear like they never existed in the first place. Your thoughts will settle, and you'll finally be able to enjoy a peaceful, stress-free life.

Throughout this book, you have learned plenty of actionable steps you can take to defeat clutter. These include methods for thinking positively more often, recognizing how past events can affect your current mental state, and rewiring your brain away from negativity. They also include tips for decluttering a busy life such as cutting back on multitasking and narrowing your focus to pursue the goals that matter the most. You learned how to declutter your relationships by limiting their number and only keeping the relationships that are positive forces in your life. You also learned the basics of redesigning your living space along the lines of a minimalist aesthetic. Through this, you can get rid of the junk that is a source of distraction and stress and train yourself to avoid making useless purchases.

Next, you learned tips and tricks for decluttering your workspace, which included getting your desk organized and avoiding interruptions, even when those interruptions come from your coworkers. Last but certainly not least, you discovered actionable steps you can take to minimize clutter from the internet by spending less time on things like social media.

Every single one of these steps is integral to living a more fulfilling life. If you allow clutter to persist in one area of your life, you guarantee that you will never truly feel well-rested, and you will never fully get rid of your stress. The best and only way to declutter your life and have the effects last is to declutter all parts of it. Through this, you will finally get your mental clutter under control so that you can pursue the goals and achievements that hold personal value to you. When your time is your own, you can choose to do whatever you wish with it.

If you follow the steps and tips for decluttering every area of your life as outlined in *How to Declutter Your Mind*, you will never have to worry about clutter again. You will be able to live a calmer, more well-rested life full of peace, good mental health, and happiness.

Thank you!

Before you go, I just wanted to say thank you for purchasing my book.

You could have picked from dozens of other books on the same topic but you took a chance and chose this one.

So, a HUGE thanks to you for getting this book and for reading all the way to the end.

Now I wanted to ask you for a small favor. ***Could you please consider posting a review on the platform? Reviews are one of the easiest ways to support the work of independent authors.***

This feedback will help me continue to write the type of books that will help you get the results you want. So if you enjoyed it, please let me know! (-:

Lastly, don't forget to grab a copy of your Free Bonus book "*7 Essential Mindfulness Habits.*"

Just go to:

https://theartofmastery.com/mindfulness

References

Ali, R., Arden-Close, E., & McAlaney, J. (2018, June 12). *Digital addiction: How technology keeps us hooked*. The Conversation. https://theconversation.com/digital-addiction-how-technology-keeps-us-hooked-97499

American Brain Society. (2019, May 1). *Stress, the silent killer*. https://americanbrainsociety.org/stress-the-silent-killer/

Bahçıvancılar, O. (n.d.). *Cluttered room with hats*. Unsplash. https://unsplash.com/photos/wh9Iojoki x8

Brickel, R. E. (n.d.). *Healthy relationships matter more than we think*. Psychalive. https://www.psychalive.org/healthy-relationships-matter/

Brown, S. (n.d.). *Clothes sorted into piles*. Unsplash.

https://unsplash.com/photos/0a7pqZm
mhuA

Carstens-Peters, G. (n.d.). *Person using a
MacBook*. Unsplash.
https://unsplash.com/photos/npxXWgQ
33ZQ

Chuttersnap. (n.d.). *Crowd of people*. Unsplash.
https://unsplash.com/photos/8I423fRM
wjM

Distel, A. (n.d.). *Facebook on desktop and
mobile*. Unsplash.
https://unsplash.com/photos/tLZhFRLj
6nY

Ducharme, J. (2018, June 5). *How to tell if
you're in a toxic relationship—And what
to do about it*. Time.
https://time.com/5274206/toxic-
relationship-signs-help/

Du Preez, P. (n.d.). *Women having a serious
conversation*. Unsplash.
https://unsplash.com/photos/F9DFuJoS
9EU

Gould, W. R. (2019, Jan. 14). *We're wired for
negativity. Here's how to keep small*

setbacks from ruining your day. NBC News. https://www.nbcnews.com/better/pop-culture/we-re-wired-negativity-here-s-how-keep-small-setbacks-ncna957201

Henderson, G. (n.d.). *"Today I am grateful" journal.* Unsplash. https://unsplash.com/photos/M4lve6jR 26E

Kurfeß, S. (n.d.). *Phone wallpaper with app notifications.* Unsplash. https://unsplash.com/photos/6lcT2kRP vnI

Madsen, I. E. H., Tripathi, M., Borritz, M., & Rugulies, R. (2014). Unnecessary work tasks and mental health: A prospective analysis of Danish human service workers. *Scandinavian Journal of Work, Environment & Health.* 40(6), 631-638. https://doi.org/10.5271/sjweh.3453

Schneider, I. (n.d.). *Passion led us here.* Unsplash. https://unsplash.com/photos/TamMbr4 okv4

Seanbatty. (2018, Apr. 18). *Two halves of your brain*. Pixabay. https://pixabay.com/illustrations/artifici al-intelligence-ai-robot-2228610/

Manasvita, S. (n.d.). *Spiral calendar*. Unsplash. https://unsplash.com/photos/9q5vptiE2 TY

McEwen, B. S. (2012, Oct. 16). Brain on stress: How the social environment gets under the skin. *Proceedings of the National Academy of Sciences of the United States of America*. 109(2), 17180-17185. https://doi.org/10.1073/pnas.112125410 9

Opfer, C. (n.d.). *Does your body really replace itself every seven years?* HowStuffWorks. https://science.howstuffworks.com/life/ cellular-microscopic/does-body-really- replace-seven-years.htm

Pappas, G. (n.d.). *Woman sleeping in bed*. Unsplash. https://unsplash.com/photos/rUc9hVE- L-E

Rothermel, E. (n.d.). *Monthly schedule.* Unsplash. https://unsplash.com/photos/FoKO4Dp XamQ

Sander, L. (2019, Jan. 20). *Time for a Kondo clean-out? Here's what clutter does to your brain and body.* The Conversation. https://theconversation.com/time-for-a-kondo-clean-out-heres-what-clutter-does-to-your-brain-and-body-109947

Scott, S. J., & Davenport, B. (2016). *Declutter your mind: How to stop worrying, relieve anxiety, and eliminate negative thinking.* Oldtown Publishing LLC.

Sheldon, J. (n.d.). *Organized coin tray.* Unsplash. https://unsplash.com/photos/Tymrm3l3 6Dk

Sikkema, K. (n.d.). *Two people holding a paper heart.* Unsplash. https://unsplash.com/photos/4le7k9XV YjE

Silviarita. (2019, Apr. 11). *Woman with a stack of books.* Pixabay.

https://pixabay.com/photos/books-woman-girl-young-people-4118058/

Sugihto, E. (2016, Aug. 23). *Dunbar's number—The law of 150*. Medium. https://medium.com/@social_archi/dunbars-number-1a8d75b94576

Vegher, D. (n.d.). *Person in a crowded library*. Unsplash. https://unsplash.com/photos/W_ZYCEUapF0

Wahid, A. (n.d.). *Painting with absolute focus*. Unsplash. https://unsplash.com/photos/VgUUGfKCuEc

Wonderlane. (n.d.). *Cluttered office room*. Unsplash. https://unsplash.com/photos/6jA6eVsRJ6Q

Yates, T. (n.d.). *A cluttered desk*. Unsplash. https://unsplash.com/photos/TQHDStvFi6o

Printed in Great Britain
by Amazon